Notting Hill Editions is an independent British publisher. The company was founded by Tom Kremer (1930–2017), champion of innovation and the man responsible for popularising the Rubik's Cube.

After a successful business career in toy invention Tom decided, at the age of eighty, to fulfil his passion for literature. In a fast-moving digital world Tom's aim was to revive the art of the essay, and to create exceptionally beautiful books that would be lingered over and cherished.

Hailed as 'the shape of things to come', the family-run press brings to print the most surprising thinkers of past and present. In an era of information-overload, these collectible pocket-size books distil ideas that linger in the mind.

Lauren Child is an English children's author and illustrator best known for her book series the Charlie and Lola picture books, which were adapted into a BAFTA-winning children's television show, for which Child was an Associate Producer; the Clarice Bean series; the Ruby Redfort novels as well as many picture books. She has also illustrated a number of books, including classics such as *Pippi Longstocking*, *The Secret Garden*, *Mary Poppins* and, most recently, *The Little Matchgirl Strikes Back* by Emma Carroll.

Child introduced Charlie and Lola in 2000 with *I Will Not Ever Never Eat a Tomato* and won the annual Kate Greenaway Medal from the Library Association for the year's most 'distinguished illustration in a book for children'. For the 50th anniversary of the Medal, a panel named it one of the top ten winning works, which comprised the shortlist for a public vote for the nation's favourite. Child was appointed Member of the Order of the British Empire (MBE) in the 2010 New Year Honours and Commander of the Order of the British Empire (CBE) in the 2021 Birthday Honours for services to children's literature. She is a former trustee of the Quentin Blake Centre for Illustration and a UNESCO Artist for Peace.

TINY FEET
A Treasury for Parents

–

Introduced by
Lauren Child

Edited by
Robin Dennis

Notting Hill Editions

Published in 2022
by Notting Hill Editions Ltd
Mirefoot, Burneside, Kendal, Cumbria LA8 9AB

Series design by FLOK Design, Berlin, Germany
Cover design by Tom Etherington
Creative Advisor: Dennis PAPHITIS

Typeset by CB Editions, London
Printed and bound by Memminger MedienCentrum,
Memmingen, Germany

Edited by Robin Dennis

A CIP record for this book is available from the British Library.

ISBN 978-1-912559-47-3

nottinghilleditions.com

Seldom 'can't,'
Seldom 'don't';
Never 'shan't,'
Never 'won't.'

– Christina G. Rossetti,
Lullaby from *Sing-Song* (1893)

A veteran in the marriage game says: 'Before
I married I had six theories about bringing
up children. Now I have six children and no
theories.'

– *The Oil Weekly* (1946)

Contents

LAUREN CHILD

– Introduction –

C hildren are not uncomplicated creatures and childhood does not cocoon from the anxieties of the world. If anything, it amplifies them, for as children we have only fragments of information and little power to put things right.

From a very tiny age, my older sister worried *constantly* that my parents were getting things 'wrong'. She – *rightly*, in my young opinion – did not keep these concerns to herself. On one occasion my sister noticed that the tax disc had unglued itself from the windscreen of our car and she became convinced that my mother's failure to display it would lead to our parents' imprisonment.

'Who will look after us then?' she furiously sobbed.

'That won't happen,' my mother tried to calm.

'You will be arrested by the police,' my sister wailed.

I absolutely took her side. Her certainty was very convincing and I could tell she properly understood exactly how these things played out. She was so hysterical that my mother had to pull over and stick the disc to the windscreen with the only thing to hand: Green Shield Stamps. As *anyone* who grew up in the seventies would know, Green Shield Stamps (reward tokens for shopping) were valuable things – collect enough and you might be able to cash them in for a set of coffee glasses – nothing my family would ever find a use for but nevertheless, desirable to own. Despite my mother's protestations that my sister was getting 'needlessly worked up', she sacrificed the stamps. Confronted by the inconsolable anxiety of my sister, there was no alternative. And after all, you are far more likely to be arrested for wanton and furious driving if you have a hysterical six-year-old screaming at you.

I rarely voiced my concerns about my mother and father's parental ineptitude – I didn't need to, my sister had that covered – I had wider worries. There was rabies for instance, a disease which caused dogs to foam at the mouth and run around looking for people to bite and infect. The rabid people would in turn foam at the mouth and run around looking for *other* people to bite, until everyone was infected and then dead. I think I had pieced together this idea from snippets I had heard on the (always on) radio and mixed them in with gory facts about the bubonic plague. But it was the proposed Channel Tunnel which tipped me over the edge; as I understood it, France (and indeed everywhere else in the world) was teeming with rabid dogs – surely the reason we banned all foreign pets from our shores. But a tunnel would obviously allow them to stampede into the country, foaming at the mouths, and that would be that: all dead. It was my aunt who coaxed this worry out of me. She kindly explained that I had got this entirely wrong and the fear vanished, only to be immediately replaced by nuclear war, not so easy to explain away.

I had watched the nuclear war survival information film at my school and none of it made any sense.

'How can taking the kitchen door off its hinges and leaning it against the hall wall prevent me getting covered in nuclear fallout?' I wondered. 'How long do I sit there eating cold baked beans directly from the tin before it is safe to come out?'

The information film told us to wait for the BBC radio announcements.

'But won't all the BBC people be sitting under their doors, eating baked beans from the tin?'

A troubling thought which grew and grew. A terror which was ultimately answered with, 'Don't worry about it.'

When I was older I understood this really meant, 'We don't know.'

No one at all had the answer because there *is* (and *was*) no answer, and my worry became (and remains): 'So just *who* is in charge?' The exact same question my much more advanced sister had been asking since she was a tiny tot.

Children are more aware of what's going on than we care to believe.

Such anxieties, big and small, from 'how to survive nuclear war' to 'how to get green felt tip off a white carpet' lurked in my childhood, but there were the other things which made up for all that. These are too many to mention and can sound a little sugary when listed, but they are there, remembered in the bones of me.

Childhood is all in the detail, the noticing: the textures on tree bark, winter's skeleton leaves, the smell of sun on stone, the click-clack of shoes on concrete, the ordinary experienced for the first time. It's life lived in close up: watching dust particles in sunlight, tracing carpet patterns with your fingers, cutting the hair of a doll because you can't resist the feeling the snipping scissors will bring. Laurie Lee expresses such things beautifully in his memoir, *Cider With Rosie*. The account of his childhood is personal to him but the sensibility surrounding it is common to many. Looking back at my childhood I find a series of moments, significant because of the emotion they held. The importance of them does not diminish with time, and for me they continue to resonate in a way my adult memories do not.

Childhood is a constant state of letting go and reaching for, of growing into and growing out of. I became consciously aware of this when, aged about ten, I was sitting on the grass with my best friend when it suddenly dawned, *this moment will not last*. That realisation brought a certain sorrow, as I recognised that time moves us on, whether we like it or not, taking us further and further away from our sixes, sevens, eights . . . each advance bringing wonder, new expectations and loss. And though, like so many children, I was egging time on, desperate for the freedoms and sophistications I thought adulthood would bring, there was another me that wanted to pull it to a stop, to be able to hold on to it a while longer. Perhaps this is where the writing comes in.

I didn't intend to become a writer, I was a drawer really, but I have always been fascinated by listening to children, their clarity of thought and the disarming straightforwardness: 'Sometimes I fall off my chair on purpose'. I love interestingly constructed phrases: 'This wood looks like handsome-man-Gretel', or 'Did you know that I fall asleep easily and stay asleep immediately?' The words often fused together or refashioned to create something more descriptive: Montessnorey (Montessori), schooliform (school uniform), *Mr Pickle Me* (*Despicable Me*). I write these down when I can, partly for my books, but usually just because I want to remember them – they are like tiny poems.

I very often write from a child's perspective *not* to *relive* childhood, but to take note. I write to understand all those thoughts that flicker in my head, by reaching back to one's *child* self, the happenings that propelled me, those things that once filled me with wonder, it is possible to puzzle out how I came to be standing where I am right now.

Before my daughter came along a question I was often asked was: 'How can you write for children, when you don't *have* any children of your own?' Perhaps as if to say, how can you possibly tune your brain to engage with the thoughts and feelings of a child, when you don't have one to study at home? It was a question that baffled me, for many reasons. Most obviously, that while there are many things I have to work hard to understand, how it *feels to be a child* is not one of these. I lived it, I felt it and I still do.

I dreaded birthday parties as a child, because you could never quite predict how things would go; would I arrive in a party dress only to find everyone was wearing jeans? Would there be a layer of marzipan lurking in an otherwise perfectly good cake, and if so, would I still be expected to eat it? If there was a game which meant getting into pairs would anyone want to be in a pair with me? Sometimes these parties turned out to be fun, sometimes I wished my parents would hurry up and get me. In my adult life I often feel the same. Weddings are particularly likely to bring back such childhood anxiety and the same utter longing for someone to fetch me home. While there are huge advantages in being an adult – you will probably decide it unnecessary to crumble your unwanted cake into your host's carpet, knowing you can instead slide it to the side of your plate and declare how *full* you are – on the downside, it is wholly unacceptable to burst into tears and sob that you *want to go home.*

There is of course no stepping back into childhood, though I still wish for it sometimes. I miss the ability to giggle with ease, to look forward to things without looking beyond them. I miss my belief that I could do pretty much anything . . . well, except for sing – my primary school teacher told me that very firmly and I have not forgotten it – be careful what you say to a child, they might believe you.

Memories of my childhood years have faded significantly, but there are those that will not be erased; among them, fittingly, the green felt tip on the white wall-to-wall carpet and the desperate attempt to scrub it away. I chopped it out with scissors in the end, and I still employ this method as a last resort.

Childhood teaches you to be resourceful, and resourcefulness is vital because there is a lot of *should* and *ought* and *can't* and *don't* about, which I suppose is why children come equipped with the power to daydream, and their optimism can be boundless. *My* aspirations all *seemed* perfectly reasonable: I would live in New York, probably in one of those large apartments overlooking that big park; I would have five or seven children. I would have hair that always did what it was meant to do, like the people on the television, and I would smell of nothing but perfume and you'd get a waft of it even after I'd left the room. I would own underwear that wasn't passed on from the Cushions (the Cushions were my Granny's next-door neighbours, and for a while all our vests and pants seemed to be provided by them, slightly gone in the elastic).

Some of these dreams remain ongoing, though the brand of perfume might have been modified, and some have been achieved (I exclusively wear my own underwear), while others have now been lost to realism, or like my desire for shiny and organised hair, remain frustratingly beyond my reach.

My friend Sofie has been more successful than I have in bringing her most ambitious childhood dreams to life. When she was little and struggling with an older brother who was not much interested in her company, she imagined herself a nicer one, and named him Soren Lorensen. He was invisible and more compliant than the original model, and he soon became a fixture in her family. Twenty years later I heard about this and was struck by her ingenuity. Faced with something she couldn't change she changed it in her head. I wrote him into a book and he found his way onto television. He has since appeared on mugs and T-shirts, there is even a band named after him – he regularly receives fan mail – and all this from the mind of a three-year-old.

DANIEL BURGESS

– *from* Advice to Parents and Children (1690) –

The French historian Philippe Ariès (1914–1984) argued that the concept of a 'childhood' – a distinct period of life during which parents nurture their children's social and psychological development – was an entirely modern invention. Ariès said that, in the past, parents primarily saw their children who survived infancy as a useful addition to the household economy. However, even in the 1600s, parents were advised to think carefully about how they treated their children, because their acts and deeds would shape them. For example, here the wildly popular Presbyterian preacher Daniel Burgess (1645–1713), known for his 'pop-gun . . . delivery', told acolytes to envelope their children in the feeling of being loved.

T ruly Parents, . . . you are your Children's first *Ministers,* as well as their *Guides* and *Rulers.* And an uncatechising Parent is a non-preaching Minister; which is so bad a Creature, that one hath said, *He thought Hell was pav'd with their Skuls.* This forget not, I beseech you; every prayer you make for your Children, that is not followed with your pains with them, is a very mocking of God and of them . . .

Be as kind as ever you can with good Conscience. Never provoke 'em, or by unnecessary hard looks, words, or acts, discourage them . . .

Convince your Children, if it be possible, that you *love* them as the apple of your eyes. And do *pray* and *labour* to make sweet their Time and Eternity. Ruling them but as God doth, drawing them with the Cords of a Man, the Bonds of Love. Shewing them by the likeness of your Government, that 'tis in God's stead that you do Rule over them. Even the God who is Love. And whose *severity* is as rare as Thunder, while his *Benignity* is as common as the day Light. Flints will break upon Wool, that will not upon Iron . . .

Parents, as you value your Children's Souls, be sure to abhor *Tyranny* on one hand, and *Anarchy* on the other. Be not so Cruel as to give them their wills in no thing, or to deny them their wills in any thing that is good. Nor so much more Cruel, as to give them their wills in every thing, or in any one sinful thing . . . Apes be not the only Bruits that hug their Whelps to death . . .

Observe carefully each Child's peculiar Temper. The difference is very great. And the need to know it is great. For how shall you else suit your dealings unto it? You must never expect to obtain your end by unsuited means. *If you are very rough with some Children, you frighten them not unto their duties but out of their wits.* Others, will scarcely learn any thing unless they be taught like the men of *Succoth,* with briars and thorns. And only a middle way, with sweetness and severity immixed, will reach others.

2

JEAN-JACQUES ROUSSEAU

– *from* Émile, or On Education
(1762) –

Widely considered to be the first treatise on pedagogy, *Émile* was an effort by Jean-Jacques Rousseau (1712–1778) to reform how children were raised. Rousseau espoused a 'natural' approach; he was a proponent of breastfeeding by the mother, rather than a wet nurse, and of letting children experiment freely in the physical world as they learned to walk, talk and look after themselves.

When it was published, many readers – including critics – imagined that *Émile* was meant as a guide for parents. Rousseau himself did not see it that way: 'It is about a new system of education, whose outline I offer up for learned scrutiny, and not a method for fathers and mothers, which I've never contemplated.' The caveat was a sly confession, because Rousseau was actually the father of five children and had raised none himself. 'Know how Jean-Jacques solved his own problems?' wrote Marjorie Mills in 1962. 'He sent [them] to a foundling home.'

Regardless, *Émile* influenced centuries of parenting guidebooks.

from Book I – Émile's infancy

Under existing conditions a man left to himself from birth would be more of a monster than the rest. Prejudice, authority, necessity, example, all the social conditions into which we are plunged, would stifle nature in him and put nothing in her place. She would be like a sapling chance sown in the midst of the highway, bent hither and thither and soon crushed by the passers-by.

Tender, anxious mother, I appeal to you. You can remove this young tree from the highway and shield it from the crushing force of social conventions. Tend and water it ere it dies. One day its fruit will reward your care. From the outset raise a wall round your child's soul; another may sketch the plan, you alone should carry it into execution.

Plants are fashioned by cultivation, man by education. If a man were born tall and strong, his size and strength would be of no good to him till he had learnt to use them; they would even harm him by preventing others from coming to his aid; left to himself he would die of want before he knew his needs. We lament the helplessness of infancy; we fail to perceive that the race would have perished had not man begun by being a child.

We are born weak, we need strength; helpless, we need aid; foolish, we need reason. All that we lack at birth, all that we need when we come to man's estate, is the gift of education.

This education comes to us from nature, from men, or from things. The inner growth of our organs and faculties is the education of nature, the use we learn to make of this growth is the education

4

of men, what we gain by our experience of our surroundings is the education of things . . .

People think only of preserving their child's life; this is not enough, he must be taught to preserve his own life when he is a man, to bear the buffets of fortune, to brave wealth and poverty, to live at need among the snows of Iceland or on the scorching rocks of Malta. In vain you guard against death; he must needs die; and even if you do not kill him with your precautions, they are mistaken. Teach him to live rather than to avoid death: life is not breath, but action, the use of our senses, our mind, our faculties, every part of ourselves which makes us conscious of our being . . .

I am told that many midwives profess to improve the shape of the infant's head by rubbing, and they are allowed to do it. Our heads are not good enough as God made them, they must be moulded outside by the nurse and inside by the philosopher . . .

The child has hardly left the mother's womb, it has hardly begun to move and stretch its limbs, when it is deprived of its freedom. It is wrapped in swaddling bands, laid down with its head fixed, its legs stretched out, and its arms by its sides; it is wound round with linen and bandages of all sorts so that it cannot move. It is fortunate if it has room to breathe, and it is laid on its side so that water which should flow from its mouth can escape, for it is not free to turn its head on one side for this purpose.

The new-born child requires to stir and stretch his limbs to free them from the stiffness resulting from being curled up so long. His limbs are stretched indeed, but he is not allowed to move them. Even the head is confined by a cap. One would think they were afraid the child should look as if it were alive . . .

It is maintained that unswaddled infants would assume faulty positions and make movements which might injure the proper development of their limbs. That is one of the empty arguments of our false wisdom which has never been confirmed by experience. Out of all the crowds of children who grow up with the full use of their limbs among nations wiser than ourselves, you never find one who hurts himself or maims himself; their movements are too feeble to be dangerous, and when they assume an injurious position, pain warns them to change it.

We have not yet decided to swaddle our kittens and puppies; are they any the worse for this neglect? Children are heavier, I admit, but they are also weaker. They can scarcely move, how could they hurt themselves? . . .

from Book II – Émile from five to twelve

We have now reached the second phase of life; infancy, strictly so-called, is over; for the words *infans* and *puer* are not synonymous. The latter includes the former, which means literally 'one who cannot speak'; thus Valerius speaks of *puerum infantem.* But I shall continue to use the word child (French *enfant*) according to the custom of our language till an age for which there is another term.

When children begin to talk they cry less. This progress is quite natural; one language supplants another. As soon as they can say 'It hurts me,' why should they cry, unless the pain is too sharp for words? If they still cry, those about them are to blame. When once Émile has said, 'It hurts me,' it will take a very sharp pain to make him cry.

If the child is delicate and sensitive, if by nature he begins to cry for nothing, I let him cry in vain and soon check his tears at their source. So long as he cries I will not go near him; I come at once when he leaves off crying. He will soon be quiet when he wants to call me, or rather he will utter a single cry. Children learn the meaning of signs by their effects; they have no other meaning for them. However much a child hurts himself when he is alone, he rarely cries, unless he expects to be heard.

Should he fall or bump his head, or make his nose bleed, or cut his fingers, I shall show no alarm, nor shall I make any fuss over him; I shall take no notice, at any rate at first. The harm is done; he must bear it; all my zeal could only frighten him more and make him more nervous. Indeed it is not the blow but the fear of it which distresses us when we are hurt. I shall spare him this suffering at least, for he will certainly regard the injury as he sees me regard it; if he finds that I hasten anxiously to him, if I pity him or comfort him, he will think he is badly hurt. If he finds I take no notice, he will soon recover himself, and will think the wound is healed when it ceases to hurt. This is the time for his first lesson in courage, and by bearing slight ills without fear we gradually learn to bear greater.

I shall not take pains to prevent Émile hurting himself; far from it, I should be vexed if he never hurt himself, if he grew up unacquainted with pain. To bear pain is his first and most useful lesson. It seems as if children were small and weak on purpose to teach them these valuable lessons without danger. The child has such a little way to fall he will not break his leg; if he knocks himself with a stick he will not break his arm; if he seizes a sharp knife he will not grasp it tight enough to make a deep wound. So far as I know, no child, left to himself, has ever been known to kill or maim itself, or even to do itself any serious harm, unless it has been foolishly left on a high place, or alone near the fire, or within reach of dangerous weapons. What is there to be said for all the paraphernalia with which the child is surrounded to shield him on every side so that he grows up at the mercy of pain, with neither courage nor experience, so that he thinks he is killed by a pin-prick and faints at the sight of blood?

With our foolish and pedantic methods we are always preventing children from learning what they could learn much better by themselves, while we neglect what we alone can teach them. Can anything be sillier than the pains taken to teach them to walk, as if there were any one who was unable to walk when he grows up through his nurse's neglect? How many we see walking badly all their life because they were ill taught?

Émile shall have no head-pads, no go-carts, no leading-strings; or at least as soon as he can put one foot before another he shall only be supported along pavements, and he shall be taken quickly across them. Instead of keeping him mewed up in a stuffy room, take him out into a meadow every day; let him run about, let him struggle and fall again and again, the oftener the better; he will learn all the sooner to pick himself up. The delights of liberty will make up for many bruises . . .

Nature provides for the child's growth in her own fashion, and this should never be thwarted. Do not make him sit still when he wants to run about, nor run when he wants to be quiet. If we did not spoil our children's wills by our blunders their desires would be free from caprice. Let them run, jump, and shout to their heart's content. All their own activities are instincts of the body for its growth in strength.

A SOCIETY OF LADIES

– *from* The Lady's Monthly Museum (1798) –

Throughout the eighteenth century, writers about child-hood, including Rousseau, viewed the first five to six years as a foundation for the more important work of formal education, or entry into training for a trade. And most of the thinking that was published came from the pens of men. As the social historian Ruth Goodman has pointed out, working wives and mothers 'commanded the smallest of financial purses', so parenting advice was published for the elite – women who had nurses and maids to help them raise their children.

This anonymous piece, from a magazine popular among Regency-era society, has a rather modern take on parenting, with its focus on developing a child's confidence and self-esteem. It stood in stark contrast to the popular *Advice to Mothers* by William Buchan, MD, a Fellow of the Royal College of Physicians. He raged against the 'baneful effects of parental tenderness', which, he said, too easily fell into 'fatal excesses of anxiety and fondness'.

I t has been a matter of some dispute, at what period of life the infant mind is capable of receiving instruction, and at what date the talk of education ought to begin. Though I am not a convert to the opinion that pride may be instilled by a new ribbon, and vanity by a gilded coral, before the child is capable of distinguishing the colour of the one, or of discriminating the make of the other, yet I am inclined to believe something may be done towards improving the disposition, even in the earliest days of childhood; and am convinced the future character is, in some degree, established before schools, or instructors, have the charge of moulding it.

Amidst the various modes of education, which either parents or preceptors are in the habit of adopting, that of *coercion* and *severity* appears to me surrounded with the greatest mischief, and big with the most fatal consequences; it cuts off that generous reciprocity which ought to subsist between the teacher and the scholar, and ingenders artifice, hatred, and deception. The *first* object in the education of a child, should be to acquire its *affection*; and the *second*, to obtain its *confidence*; but how are either to be hoped for, if severity chill, or coercion bind, the soft affections of its feeling heart? – If a child is in the habit of considering its mother, or governess, as a *rigid judge*, rather than a *tender friend*, how can it be supposed to act with that ingenuous confidence which is so essentially necessary for its future welfare? – Or how is it possible for an instructor to form or improve that mind, the secret movements of which they are wholly unacquainted with?

The keeping children in a constant state of subjection and dependence, is one of the most fatal errors a parent can fall into; for by this tyrannic sway over their minds and persons, the former becomes enervated, and the latter dwindles into a mere machine.

The springs of the mind, like the joints of the body, become inactive by disuse; and unless the former has something to simulate, and draw them forth, they naturally sink into listlessness or apathy. – If the social affections are allowed to be the chief awakeners of man, with how much greater degree of stimulus must they act upon childhood? The most likely thing to expand the youthful mind, and fire it with an ardent love of virtue, is *praise*; for unless a child is taught to entertain a *high opinion for itself*, or to believe others will value it for its amiable qualities, it will feel no temptation to cultivate virtue, and no desire to act upon principle. But in teaching a child to respect *itself*, it ought carefully to be informed *why* it is *respectable*; it ought to be told that nature had endowed it with faculties capable of the most exalted pursuits, and that by destining each to their proper use, it might in time become a noble being! – It ought early to be inspired with a *love* of *truth*, a *detestation* of *falsehood*, and a perfect abhorrence of *hypocrisy* and *deception*.

Few circumstances can be attended with such pernicious consequences as an attempt to impose upon a child's understanding; for if parents expect frankness and sincerity in their children, they ought carefully to avoid every species of artifice; and instead of alluring them by *deception*, incite them by principle.

JOHANN HEINRICH PESTALOZZI

– *from* How Gertrude Teaches Her Children (1800) –

Starting in 1770, the Swiss educator Johann Heinrich
Pestalozzi (1746–1827) had used *Émile* as a guidebook
for raising his own son. He decided Rousseau's ideas
needed some rethinking if they were to work in practice.
No parent had enough time to manage a child's development, even if the child was left to develop naturally. At
the same time, a parent's touch was important.

First at an orphanage at Stans and later at his teachers'
school at Burgdorf, Pestalozzi set out to make schools
more like home – a safe place for young children to
explore the world. Children played with real-world
objects, familiarising themselves with their form and
function through hands-on learning. Among his teacher-
students was Friedrich Froebel, who established the first
kindergarten.

F rom the moment that a mother takes a child
upon her lap, she teaches him. She brings
nearer to his sense what nature has scattered afar
off over large areas and in confusion, and makes
the action of receiving sense-impressions and the
knowledge derived from them, easy, pleasant, and
delightful to him.

The mother, weak and untrained, follows Nature

14

without help or guidance, and knows not what she is doing. She does not intend to teach, she intends only to quiet the child, to occupy him. But, nevertheless, in her pure simplicity, she follows the high course of Nature without knowing what *Nature* does through *her*; and Nature does very much through her. In this way she opens the world to the child. She makes him ready to use his senses, and prepares for the early development of his attention and power of observation . . .

How do I come to love, trust, thank, and obey men? How come those feelings in my nature on which human love, human gratitude, human confidence rest, and those activities by which obedience is formed? And I find: *That they have their chief source in the relations that exist between the baby and his mother.*

The mother is forced by the power of animal instinct to tend her child, feed him, protect and please him. She does this. She satisfies his wants, she removes anything unpleasant, she comes to the help of his helplessness. The child is cared for, is pleased. *The germ of love is developed in him.*

Now put an object that he has never seen before his eyes; he is astonished, frightened, he cries. The mother presses him to her bosom, dandles him, and diverts him. He leaves off crying, but his eyes are still wet. The object appears again. The mother takes him into her sheltering arms and smiles at him again. Now he weeps no more. He returns his mother's smile with clear unclouded eyes. *The germ of trust is developed in him.*

The mother hastens to his cradle at his every need. She is there at the hour of hunger, she gives him drink in the hour of thirst. When he hears her step he is quiet, when he sees her he stretches out his hands. His eye is cast on her breast. He is satisfied. Mother, and being satisfied, are one and the same thought to him. *He is grateful.*

The germs of love, trust and gratitude soon grow. The child knows his mother's step; he smiles at her shadow. He loves those who are like her; a creature like his mother is a good creature to him. He smiles at his mother's face, at all human faces; he loves those who are dear to his mother. Whom his mother embraces, he embraces; whom his mother kisses, he kisses too. *The germ of human love, of brotherly love is developed in him.*

Obedience in its origin is an activity whose driving-wheel is opposed to the first inclinations of animal nature. Its cultivation rests on art. It is not a simple result of pure instinct, but it is closely connected with it. Its first stage is distinctly instinctive. As *want* precedes love, *nourishment* gratitude, and *care* trust, so *passionate desire* precedes obedience. The child screams before he waits, he is impatient before he obeys. Patience is developed before obedience; he only becomes obedient through patience. The first manifestations of this virtue are simply passive; they arise generally from a consciousness of hard necessity. But this, too, is first developed on the mother's lap. The child must wait until she opens her breast to him; he must wait until she takes him up. *Active* obedience develops much later, and later still, the consciousness that it is good for him to obey his mother.

ELLA CARA DELORIA

– *from* Waterlily (*c.*1845) –

Ella Cara Deloria (1889–1971), also called Aŋpétu Wašté
Wiŋ, was born in White Swan in the Dakota Territory,
and grew up on the Standing Rock Indian Reservation
at Wakpala, South Dakota. While studying at Teachers College, Columbia University, in New York, she met
anthropologist Franz Boas and joined his team, along
with Margaret Mead and Ruth Benedict, researching
Native cultures and linguistics.

In the 1940s, she began work on her novel, *Waterlily*,
the story of young mother Blue Bird and her daughter.
The novel drew upon Deloria's anthropological fieldwork, as well as stories handed down to her by her
father's Sioux family, to capture life among the Sioux a
century earlier. Sadly, she did not get to see the novel
published in her lifetime.

J ust what was it her grandmother once told a
woman – something about the best position to
induce an easy birth? Or was it quick birth? What
was it, anyway? She groped for it in her confused
mind. Suddenly it came like a flash. And with it
something else the grandmother once said: 'No
woman cries out like a baby; people ridicule that.
To carry a child is an awesome thing. If one is old
enough to bear a child, one is old enough to endure
in silence.'

Blue Bird clung to those words with desperate tenacity and allowed not a moan to escape her, though she was alone. An eternity passed – and then, the child was a girl. Of that she was vaguely aware as she picked it up from the soft grass on which it lay and fumbled for her knife in its case hanging on her belt. Cleanly and quickly she cut the cord, as old wives said it should be cut. She herself had never beheld such a thing. Unmarried young women did not witness births.

Still dazed, she wrapped her child in a fawn-skin, which she had prepared in secret, working it long hours at a time to render it white and pliable and soft. She had kept it with her against this hour. Next she changed to a fresh gown, wrapped the placenta and cord in the discarded one, and tied it in a neat bundle. Then, stretching with superhuman effort, she settled it securely into the fork of a tree, well beyond the reach of desecrating animals. You should always do this, for every newborn child, that it might grow up straight-limbed and clear-minded. Everyone knew that; it was the ancient law.

At the water's edge she knelt to wash her stained hands. Then, hardly knowing why, she rained a few drops gently on the little face that fitted nicely into the hollow of her hand. But, try as she would, she could not concentrate on the wonder she held there. All around the waterlilies in full bloom seemed to pull her eyes to them irresistibly, until she turned her gaze on them with exaggerated astonishment. How beautiful they were! How they made you open your eyes wider and wider the longer you looked – as if daring you to penetrate their outer shape and comprehend their spirit. She glanced from one to another, and suddenly it was impossible to distinguish them from her baby's face. A new sensation welled up within her, almost choking her, and she was articulate for the first time. 'My daughter! My daughter!' she cried. 'How beautiful you are! As beautiful as the waterlilies. You too are a waterlily, *my* waterlily.' She sobbed with joy . . .

Any family could maintain itself adequately as long as the father was a good hunter and the mother an industrious woman. But socially that was not enough; ideally it must be part of a larger family, constituted of related households, called *tioyospaye* ('group of tipis'). In the camp circle such groups placed their tipis side by side where they would be within easy reach for cooperative living. In their closeness lay such strength and social importance as no single family, however able, could have wished to achieve entirely by its own efforts.

In the atmosphere of that larger group, all adults were responsible for the safety and happiness of their collective children. The effect on the growing child was a feeling of security and self-assurance, and that was all to the good. Almost from the beginning everyone could declare, 'I am not afraid; I have relatives.' To be cast out from one's relatives was literally to be lost. To return to them was to recover one's rightful haven.

It was to such a haven that Blue Bird finally came back. It was where she belonged and where her child belonged. It was important for her daughter to grow up with backing, in informal association with the girls – her cousins and sisters – and in a respect relationship with her brothers and male cousins, who would stand back of her, ready if she should need help . . .

The months passed unnoticed, with the daily activities of the relatives and with [her daughter], the ever-changing Waterlily, for a preoccupation, and almost before Blue Bird realized it, her child was in the creeping stage, very active, into everything, and required constant watching. But one day when the grandmother was out and there was outside work for Blue Bird to do, she placed Waterlily in the center of a huge spread-out buffalo robe and barricaded her all around with long, hard pillows of skin stuffed with deer hair. She handed Waterlily her wooden playthings, the ring 'teeth-maker' and the little turtle with its entire back worked in colors to simulate the design on a real turtle. In a peculiar sense this was Waterlily's very own turtle, for was she herself not inside of it? Somewhere in the stuffing of down was the bit of withered navel that fell from her shortly after her birth. When she was old enough to wear an elaborately decorated gown, this turtle would be attached to the center back of her belt brooch as an ornament and as a talisman ensuring long life to her. Until then it was a toy.

In no time at all Waterlily had lost all her trinkets in the shaggy fur and tossed her beloved turtle overboard and then climbed easily over the pillows to retrieve it. But on the way she stopped to put a bit of charcoal into her mouth. Luckily, the fireplace was cold. She first examined the charcoal minutely, while a little boy of perhaps six years stood watching her at the entrance, smiling but anxious, seeing what she was about. The instant she took the charcoal to her mouth he moved swiftly to her and fell on one knee, coaxing her to give it up. Waterlily quickly clamped her lips together – for keeps.

'Ah! That's bad. Here, spit,' he entreated her, cupping a hand under her chin to catch it. She looked at him genially and her round cheeks curved up in friendliness, but her mouth remained tightly pursed. 'Well,' he said, 'I'll make you laugh and then you will open your mouth.' He made funny faces and funny noises while the child stared at him in wonder. No use. He must try another tack. He would be a wild pony.

Like all little boys, he loved horses and knew their actions well. He could imitate them, in his own fashion. Suddenly he was a most spirited one, a wild bucking horse that could throw and maybe even kill his rider. He assumed a four-footed position and jumped unbelievably high, straight up, and landed on all fours in almost the same spot. Then he reared; he raised his forelegs high; he humped his back menacingly and turned round and round very fast. Let any rider try to stay on!

Waterlily was charmed but she did not give up the charcoal. Maybe she had already swallowed it. But try one more thing. The boy stopped directly before her and looked at her fiercely and then shook his wild, disheveled head from side to side and up and down. Finally, breathing very loud, he neighed just like a horse. It was the neighing that did it. Waterlily screamed merrily and the charcoal fell out.

From that day on the two children were fast friends. The boy came to see her often and played with her, patiently sitting by and picking up her toys, only to have her hurl them out again. It was a game with them.

The boy, who said his name was Little Chief, was an appealing child with gentle ways that pleased Blue Bird. She might have guessed what she later learned, that he was 'grandmother raised,' for his language was precocious and amusingly quaint, copied from the talk of elderly people, who often used obsolete words and phrases. He used his kinship terms readily and well, a sign of good manners.

Obviously he had been carefully trained, as only painstaking grandparents could train a child – with quiet suasion. 'That is not done, grandchild,' they said quietly, or 'Nobody does that,' meaning 'and neither ought you.' No cross words, no whipping, just those simple words of correction, in kindly tones, were remarkably effective. The very calmness of grandparents soothed a child and made him inclined to obey.

ISABELLA BEETON

– *from* Beeton's Book of Household Management (1861) –

Beeton's Book of Household Management was the bible of
the middle-class housewife on both sides of the Atlantic for more than fifty years. In the first edition, Isabella
Beeton (1836–1865) collected more than 936 pages of
cookery advice and recipes before turning her sights on
other aspects of the household, including hiring staff
and – finally – the challenges of raising an infant. She
was just 25 years old, mother of one infant who had died
at 3 months and a toddler who would die within a year.
So her focus on infants' health and safety is understandable. At the same time, she clearly believed health and
safety were built upon a foundation of parental love.

T he infantine management of children, like the
mother's love for her offspring, seems to be
born with the child, and to be a direct intelligence
of Nature. It may thus, at first sight, appear as inconsistent and presumptuous to tell a woman how to
rear her infant as to instruct her in the manner of
loving it. Yet, though Nature is unquestionably the
best nurse, Art makes so admirable a foster-mother,
that no sensible woman, in her novitiate of parent,
would refuse the admonitions of art, or the teachings of experience, to consummate her duties of

nurse. It is true that, in a civilized state of society, few young wives reach the epoch that makes them mothers without some insight, traditional or practical, into the management of infants; consequently, the cases wherein a woman is left to her own unaided intelligence, or what, in such a case, may be called instinct, and obliged to trust to the promptings of nature alone for the well-being of her child, are very rare indeed. Again, every woman is not gifted with the same physical ability for the harassing duties of a mother; and though Nature, as a general rule, has endowed all female creation with the attributes necessary to that most beautiful and, at the same time, holiest function – the healthy rearing of their offspring – the cases are sufficiently numerous to establish the exception, where the mother is either physically or socially incapacitated from undertaking these most pleasing duties herself, and where, consequently, she is compelled to trust to adventitious aid for those natural benefits which are at once the mother's price and delight to render to her child . . .

All children come into the world in the same imploring helplessness, with the same general organization and wants, and demanding either from the newly-awakened mother's love, or from the memory of motherly feeling in the nurse, or the common appeals of humanity in those who undertake the earliest duties of an infant, the same assistance and protection, and the same fostering care . . .

We, undoubtedly, believe that crying, to a certain extent, is not only conducive to health, but positively necessary to the full development and physical economy of the infant's being. But though holding this opinion, we are far from believing that a child does not very often cry from pain, thirst, want of food, and attention to its personal comfort; but there is as much difference in the tone and expression of a child's cry as in the notes of an adult's voice; and the mother's ear will not be long in discriminating between the sharp peevish whine of irritation and fever, and the louder intermitting cry that characterizes the want of warmth and sleep. All these shades of expression in the child's inarticulate voice every nurse *should* understand, and every mother will soon teach herself to interpret them with an accuracy equal to language.

There is no part of a woman's duty to her child that a young mother should so soon make it her business to study, as the voice of her infant, and the language conveyed in its cry. The study is neither hard nor difficult; a close attention to its tone, and the expression of the baby's features, are the two most important points .... The key to both the mother will find in her own heart, and the knowledge of her success in the comfort and smile of her infant. We have two reasons – both strong ones – for urging on mothers the imperative necessity of early making themselves acquainted with the nature and wants of their child: the first, that when left to the entire responsibility of the baby, after the departure of the nurse, she may be able to undertake her new duties with more confidence than if left to her own resources and mother's instinct, without a clue to guide her through the mysteries of those calls that vibrate through every nerve of her nature; and, secondly, that she may be able to guard her child from the nefarious practices of unprincipled nurses, who, while calming the mother's mind with false statements as to the character of the baby's cries, rather than lose their rest, or devote that time which would remove the cause of suffering, administer, behind the curtains, those deadly narcotics which, while stupefying Nature into sleep, insure for herself a night of many unbroken hours . . .

We must strenuously warn all mothers on *no* account to allow the nurse to sleep with the baby, never herself to lay down with it by her side for a night's rest, never to let it sleep in the parents' bed, and on no account keep it, longer than absolutely necessary, confined in an atmosphere loaded with the breath of many adults . . .

Mothers, in the fulness of their affection, believe there is no harbour, sleeping or awake, where their infants can be so secure from all possible or probably danger as in their own arms; yet we should astound our readers if we told them the statistical number of infants who, in despite of their motherly solicitude and love, are annually killed, unwittingly, by such parents themselves . . . The only possible excuse that can be urged, either by nurse or mother, for this culpable practice, is the plea of imparting warmth to the infant. But this can always be effected by an extra blanket in the child's crib, or, if the weather is particularly cold, by a bottle of hot water enveloped in flannel and placed at the child's feet; while all the objections already urged – as derivable from animal heat imparted by actual contact – are entirely obviated. There is another evil attending the sleeping together of the mother and infant, which, as far as regards the latter, we consider quite as formidable, though not so immediate as the others, and is always followed by more or less mischief to the mother. The evil we now allude to is that most injurious practice of letting the child *suck* after the mother has *fallen asleep*, a custom that naturally results from the former, and which, as we have already said, is injurious to both mother and child. It is injurious to the infant by allowing it, without control, to imbibe to distension a fluid sluggishly secreted and deficient in those vital principles which the want of mental energy, and of the sympathetic appeals of the child on the mother, so powerfully produce on the secreted nutriment, while the mother wakes in a state of clammy exhaustion, with giddiness, dimness of sight, nausea, loss of appetite, and a dull aching pain through the back and between the shoulders. In fact, she wakes languid and unrefreshed from her sleep, with febrile symptoms and hectic flushes, caused by her baby vampire, who, while dragging from her her health and strength, has excited in itself a set of symptoms directly opposite, but fraught with the same injurious consequences – 'functional derangement'.

CHARLES DARWIN

– *from* A Biographical Sketch of an Infant (1877) –

Naturalist Charles Darwin (1809–1882) trained his scientific eye on everything around him, including his own
children. He kept a detailed diary of the development
of his first son, William Erasmus, from his birth in 1839
until 1841. In his *Autobiography* Darwin explained: 'I at
once commenced to make notes on the first dawn of the
various expressions which he exhibited, for I felt convinced, even at this early period, that the most complex
and fine shades of expression must all have had a gradual
and natural origin.' He gleaned observations from the
diary for this article, published in the journal *Mind*,
nearly four decades later, after his theory of evolution
had won him fame.

A very interesting account of the mental development of an infant . . . has led me to look
over a diary which I kept thirty-seven years ago with
respect to one of my own infants. I had excellent
opportunities for close observation, and wrote down
at once whatever was observed. My chief object was
expression, and my notes were used in my book on
this subject; but as I attended to some other points,
my observations may possibly possess some little
interest . . . I feel sure, from what I have seen with

my own infants, that the period of development of the several faculties will be found to differ considerably in different infants.

During the first seven days various reflex actions, namely sneezing, hickuping, yawning, stretching, and of course sucking and screaming, were well performed by my infant. On the seventh day, I touched the naked sole of his foot with a bit of paper, and he jerked it away, curling at the same time his toes, like a much older child when tickled. The perfection of these reflex movements shows that the extreme imperfection of the voluntary ones is not due to the state of the muscles or of the coordinating centres, but to that of the seat of the will. At this time, though so early, it seemed clear to me that a warm soft hand applied to his face excited a wish to suck. This must be considered as a reflex or an instinctive action, for it is impossible to believe that experience and association with the touch of his mother's breast could so soon have come into play. During the first fortnight he often started on hearing any sudden sound, and blinked his eyes. The same fact was observed with some of my other infants within the first fortnight. Once, when he was 66 days old, I happened to sneeze, and he started violently, frowned, looked frightened, and cried rather badly: for an hour afterwards he was in a state which would be called nervous in an older person, for every slight noise made him start. A few days before this same date, he first started at an object suddenly seen; but for a long time afterwards sounds made him start and wink his eyes much more frequently than did sight; thus when 114 days old, I shook a paste-board box with comfits in it near his face and he started, whilst the same box when empty or any other object shaken as near or much nearer to his face produced no effect. We may infer from these several facts that the winking of the eyes, which manifestly serves to protect them, had not been acquired through experience. Although so sensitive to sound in a general way, he was not able even when 124 days old easily to recognise whence a sound proceeded, so as to direct his eyes to the source.

With respect to vision, – his eyes were fixed on a candle as early as the 9th day, and up to the 45th day nothing else seemed thus to fix them; but on the 49th day his attention was attracted by a bright-coloured tassel, as was shown by his eyes becoming fixed and the movements of his arms ceasing. It was surprising how slowly he acquired the power of following with his eyes an object if swinging at all rapidly; for he could not do this well when seven and a half months old. At the age of 32 days he perceived his mother's bosom when three or four inches from it, as was shown by the protrusion of his lips and his eyes becoming fixed; but I much doubt whether this had any connection with vision; he certainly had not touched the bosom. Whether he was guided through

smell or the sensation of warmth or through association with the position in which he was held, I do not
at all know.

The movements of his limbs and body were
for a long time vague and purposeless, and usually
performed in a jerking manner; but there was one
exception to this rule, namely, that from a very early
period, certainly long before he was 40 days old, he
could move his hands to his own mouth. When 77
days old, he took the sucking bottle (with which he
was partly fed) in his right hand, whether he was
held on the left or right arm of his nurse, and he
would not take it in his left hand until a week later
although I tried to make him do so; so that the right
hand was a week in advance of the left. Yet this
infant afterwards proved to be left-handed, the tendency being no doubt inherited – his grandfather,
mother, and a brother having been or being left-
handed. When between 80 and 90 days old, he drew
all sorts of objects into his mouth, and in two or
three weeks' time could do this with some skill; but
he often first touched his nose with the object and
then dragged it down into his mouth. After grasping
my finger and drawing it to his mouth, his own hand
prevented him from sucking it; but on the 114th day,
after acting in this manner, he slipped his own hand
down so that he could get the end of my finger into
his mouth. This action was repeated several times,
and evidently was not a chance but a rational one . . .

When four months old, he often looked intently at his own hands and other objects close to him, and in doing so the eyes were turned much inwards, so that he often squinted frightfully. In a fortnight after this time (i.e. 132 days old) I observed that if an object was brought as near to his face as his own hands were, he tried to seize it, but often failed; and he did not try to do so in regard to more distant objects. I think there can be little doubt that the convergence of his eyes gave him the clue and excited him to move his arms. Although this infant thus began to use his hands at an early period, he showed no special aptitude in this respect, for when he was 2 years and 4 months old, he held pencils, pens, and other objects far less neatly and efficiently than did his sister who was then only 14 months old, and who showed great inherent aptitude in handling anything.

Anger. – It was difficult to decide at how early an age anger was felt; on his eighth day he frowned and wrinkled the skin round his eyes before a crying fit, but this may have been due to pain or distress, and not to anger. When about ten weeks old, he was given some rather cold milk and he kept a slight frown on his forehead all the time that he was sucking, so that he looked like a grown-up person made cross from being compelled to do something which he did not like. When nearly four months old, and perhaps much earlier, there could be no doubt, from the manner in which the blood gushed into his whole face and scalp, that he easily got into a violent passion. A small cause sufficed; thus, when a little over seven months old, he screamed with rage because a lemon slipped away and he could not seize it with his hands. When eleven months old, if a wrong plaything was given to him, he would push it away and beat it; I presume that the beating was an instinctive sign of anger, like the snapping of the jaws by a young crocodile just out of the egg, and not that he imagined he could hurt the plaything. When two years and three months old, he became a great adept at throwing books or sticks, &c., at anyone who offended him; and so it was with some of my other sons. On the other hand, I could never see a trace of such aptitude in my infant daughters; and this makes me think that a tendency to throw objects is inherited by boys.

Fear. – This feeling probably is one of the earliest which is experienced by infants, as shown by their starting at any sudden sound when only a few weeks old, followed by crying. Before the present one was 4½ months old I had been accustomed to make close to him many strange and loud noises, which were all taken as excellent jokes, but at this period I one day made a loud snoring noise which I had never done before; he instantly looked grave and then burst out crying. Two or three days afterwards, I made through forgetfulness the same noise with the same result. About the same time (viz. on the 137th day) I approached with my back towards him and then stood motionless; he looked very grave and much surprised, and would soon have cried, had I not turned round; then his face instantly relaxed into a smile. It is well known how intensely older children suffer from vague and undefined fears, as from the dark, or in passing an obscure corner in a large hall, &c. I may give as an instance that I took the child in question, when 2¼ years old, to the Zoological Gardens, and he enjoyed looking at all the animals which were like those that he knew, such as deer, antelopes &c., and all the birds, even the ostriches, but was much alarmed at the various larger animals in cages. He often said afterwards that he wished to go again, but not to see 'beasts in houses'; and we could in no manner account for this fear . . .

Affection. – This probably arose very early in life, if we may judge by his smiling at those who had charge of him when under two months old; though I had no distinct evidence of his distinguishing and recognising anyone, until he was nearly four months old. When nearly five months old, he plainly showed his wish to go to his nurse. But he did not spontaneously exhibit affection by overt acts until a little above a year old, namely, by kissing several times his nurse who had been absent for a short time. With respect to the allied feeling of sympathy, this was clearly shown at 6 months and 11 days by his melancholy face, with the corners of his mouth well depressed, when his nurse pretended to cry. Jealousy was plainly exhibited when I fondled a large doll, and when I weighed his infant sister, he being then 15½ months old. Seeing how strong a feeling jealousy is in dogs, it would probably be exhibited by infants at an earlier age than that just specified, if they were tried in a fitting manner.

Association of Ideas, Reason, &c. – . . . When five months old, associated ideas arising independently of any instruction became fixed in his mind; thus as soon as his hat and cloak were put on, he was very cross if he was not immediately taken out of doors. When exactly seven months old, he made the great step of associating his nurse with her name, so that if I called it out he would look round for her. Another infant used to amuse himself by shaking his head laterally: we praised and imitated him, saying 'Shake your head'; and when he was seven months old, he would sometimes do so on being told without any other guide. During the next four months the former infant associated many things and actions with words; thus when asked for a kiss he would protrude his lips and keep still, – would shake his head and say in a scolding voice 'Ah' to the coal-box or a little spilt water, &c., which he had been taught to consider as dirty . . . When a few days over nine months, he learnt spontaneously that a hand or other object causing a shadow to fall on the wall in front of him was to be looked for behind . . . The facility with which associated ideas due to instruction and others spontaneously arising were acquired, seemed to me by far the most strongly marked of all the distinctions between the mind of an infant and that of the cleverest full-grown dog that I have ever known. What a contrast does the mind of an infant present to that of the pike, described by Professor Möbius, who during three whole months dashed and stunned himself against a glass partition which separated him from some minnows . . .

Means of Communication. – The noise of crying or rather of squalling, as no tears are shed for a long time, is of course uttered in an instinctive manner, but serves to show that there is suffering. After a time the sound differs according to the cause, such as hunger or pain. This was noticed when this infant was eleven weeks old, and I believe at an earlier age in another infant. Moreover, he appeared soon to learn to begin crying voluntarily, or to wrinkle his face in the manner proper to the occasion, so as to show that he wanted something. When 46 days old, he first made little noises without any meaning to please himself, and these soon became varied. An incipient laugh was observed on the 113th day, but much earlier in another infant. At this date I thought, as already remarked, that he began to try to imitate sounds, as he certainly did at a considerably later period. When five and a half months old, he uttered an articulate sound 'da' but without any meaning attached to it. When a little over a year old, he used gestures to explain his wishes; to give a simple instance, he picked up a bit of paper and giving it to me pointed to the fire, as he had often seen and liked to see paper burnt. At exactly the age of a year, he made the great step of inventing a word for food, namely *mum*, but what led him to it I did not discover.

ROBERT LOUIS STEVENSON

– *from* Child's Play (1878) –

Best known for his novels *Treasure Island*, *Kidnapped* and *Strange Case of Dr Jekyll and Mr Hyde*, Robert Louis Stevenson (1850–1894) also wrote numerous works of non-fiction, including essays on play and make-believe published in the book *Child's Play* and *The Cornhill Magazine*. Anticipating numerous twentieth-century theorists, he described the interior life of the child, where what is seen in the mind begs to be enacted, as the child learns how to operate in the world. In later life, he said of his own youth: 'I have three powerful impressions of my childhood: my sufferings when I was sick, my delights in convalescence at my grandfather's manse of Colinton, near Edinburgh, and the unnatural activity of my mind after I was in bed at night.'

We grown people can tell ourselves a story, give and take strokes until the bucklers ring, ride far and fast, marry, fall, and die; all the while sitting quietly by the fire or lying prone in bed. This is exactly what a child cannot do, or does not do, at least, when he can find anything else. He works all with lay figures and stage properties. When his story comes to the fighting, he must rise, get something by way of a sword and have a set-to with a piece of furniture, until he is out of breath. When he comes to ride with the king's pardon, he must bestride a chair, which he will so hurry and belabour and on which he will so furiously demean himself, that the messenger will arrive, if not bloody with spurring, at least fiery red with haste. If his romance involves an accident upon a cliff, he must clamber in person about the chest of drawers and fall bodily upon the carpet, before his imagination is satisfied. Lead soldiers, dolls, all toys, in short, are in the same category and answer the same end. Nothing can stagger a child's faith; he accepts the clumsiest substitutes and can swallow the most staring incongruities. The chair he has just been besieging as a castle, or valiantly cutting to the ground as a dragon, is taken away for the accommodation of a morning visitor, and he is nothing abashed; he can skirmish by the hour with a stationary coal-scuttle; in the midst of the enchanted pleasance, he can see, without sensible shock, the gardener soberly digging potatoes for the day's dinner. He can make abstraction of whatever does not fit into his fable; and he puts his eyes into his pocket, just as we hold our noses in an unsavoury lane . . .

In the child's world of dim sensation, play is all in all. 'Making believe' is the gist of his whole life, and he cannot so much as take a walk except in character. I could not learn my alphabet without some suitable *mise-en-scène*, and had to act a business man in an office before I could sit down to my book. Will you kindly question your memory, and find out how much you did, work or pleasure, in good faith and soberness, and for how much you had to cheat yourself with some invention? I remember, as though it were yesterday, the expansion of spirit, the dignity and self-reliance, that came with a pair of mustachios in burnt cork, even when there was none to see. Children are even content to forego what we call the realities, and prefer the shadow to the substance. When they might be speaking intelligibly together, they chatter senseless gibberish by the hour, and are quite happy because they are making believe to speak French. I have said already how even the imperious appetite of hunger suffers itself to be gulled and led by the nose with the fag end of an old song. And it goes deeper than this: when children are together even a meal is felt as an interruption in the business of life; and they must find some imaginative sanction, and tell themselves some sort of story, to account for, to colour, to render entertaining, the simple processes of eating and drinking. What wonderful fancies I have heard evolved out of the pattern upon tea-cups! – from which there followed a code of rules and a whole world of excitement, until tea-drinking began to take rank as a game. When my cousin and I took our porridge of a morning, we had a device to enliven the course of the meal. He ate his with sugar, and explained it to be a country continually buried under snow. I took mine with milk, and explained it to be a country suffering gradual inundation. You can imagine us exchanging bulletins; how here was an island still unsubmerged, here a valley not yet covered with snow; what inventions were made; how his population lived in cabins on perches and travelled on stilts, and how mine was always in boats; how the interest grew furious, as the last corner of safe ground was cut off on all sides and grew smaller every moment; and how in fine, the food was of altogether secondary importance, and might even have been nauseous, so long as we seasoned it with these dreams . . .

To think of such a frame of mind, is to become disquieted about the bringing up of children. Surely they dwell in a mythological epoch, and are not the contemporaries of their parents. What can they think of them? what can they make of these bearded or petticoated giants who look down upon their games? who move upon a cloudy Olympus, following unknown designs apart from rational enjoyment? who profess the tenderest solicitude for children, and yet every now and again reach down out of their altitude and terribly vindicate the prerogatives of age? Off goes the child, corporally smarting, but morally rebellious. Were there ever such unthinkable deities as parents? I would give a great deal to know what, in nine cases out of ten, is the child's unvarnished feeling. A sense of past cajolery; a sense of personal attraction, at best very feeble; above all, I should imagine, a sense of terror for the untried residue of mankind go to make up the attraction that he feels. No wonder, poor little heart, with such a weltering world in front of him, if he clings to the hand he knows! The dread irrationality of the whole affair, as it seems to children, is a thing we are all too ready to forget. 'O, why,' I remember passionately wondering, 'why can we not all be happy and devote ourselves to play?' And when children do philosophise, I believe it is usually to very much the same purpose.

One thing, at least, comes very clearly out of these considerations; that whatever we are to expect at the hands of children, it should not be any peddling exactitude about matters of fact. They walk in a vain show, and among mists and rainbows; they are passionate after dreams and unconcerned about realities; speech is a difficult art not wholly learned; and there is nothing in their own tastes or purposes to teach them what we mean by abstract truthfulness . . .

It would be easy to leave them in their native cloudland, where they figure so prettily – pretty like flowers and innocent like dogs. They will come out of their gardens soon enough, and have to go into offices and the witness-box. Spare them yet a while, O conscientious parent! Let them doze among their playthings yet a little! for who knows what a rough, warfaring existence lies before them in the future?

JAMES SULLY

– *from* The Questioning Age (1894) –

A founding member of the British Psychological Society, James Sully (1842–1923) has been called 'one of the
moving spirits behind the child study movement'. Like
Darwin, his ideas were informed by his own son, whose
psychological development he closely observed – fore-
most as a scientist rather than a father – over the first six
years. This essay was one of a multipart series entitled
'Studies of Childhood', first published for a general read-
ership in *Popular Science* magazine and later collected in
book form.

T he child's first vigorous effort to understand
the things about him may be roughly dated at
the end of the third year, and it is noteworthy that
this synchronizes with the advent of the questioning
age . . .

A common theory peculiarly favoured by ignorant nurses and mothers is that children's questioning is a studied annoyance. The child has come to
the use of words, and with all a child's 'cussedness'
proceeds to torment the ears of those about him.
There are signs, however, of a change of view on this
point. The fact that the questioning follows on the
heels of the reasoning impulse might tell us that it is
connected with the throes which the young under-

standing has to endure in its first collision with a tough and baffling world. The question is the outcome of ignorance coupled with a belief in a possible knowledge. It aims at filling up a gap in the child's knowledge, at getting from the fuller knowledge of another some light on the scrappy, unsatisfying information about things which is all that his own observation can gather, or all that others' half-understood words have managed to communicate. It is the outcome of intellectual craving – a demand for food. But it is much more than an expression of need. Just as the child's articulate demand for food implies that he knows what food is, and that it is obtainable, so the question implies that the little questioner knows what he needs, and in what direction to look for it. The simplest form of question – e.g., What is this flower, this insect? – shows that the child, by a half-conscious process of reflection and reasoning, has found his way to the truth that things have their qualities, their belongings, their names.

Questioning may take various directions. A good deal of the child's catechising of his long-suffering mother is prompted by thirst for fact. The typical form of this line of questioning is 'What?' The motive here is to gain possession of some fact which will connect itself with and supplement a fact already known. How old is Rover? Where was Rover born? Who was his father? What is that dog's name? What sort of hair had you when you were a little girl? These are samples of the questioning activity by the help of which the little inquirer tries to make up his connected wholes – to see things with his imagination in their proper attachment and order. And how greedily and pertinaciously the small people will follow up their questioning, flying, as it often looks, wildly enough from point to point, yet gathering from every answer some new contribution to their ideas of things! A boy of three years and nine months would thus attack his mother: 'What does frogs eat, and mice, and birds, and butterflies? and what does they do? and what is their names? What is all their houses' names? What does they call their streets and places?' etc . . .

One feature in this fact-gleaning kind of question is the great store which the child sets by the name of a thing. M. Compayré has pointed out that the form of question, 'What is this?' often means 'What is it called?' The child's unformulated theory seems to be that everything has its own individual name. The little boy just spoken of explained to his mother that he thought all the frogs, the mice, the birds, and the butterflies had names given to them by their mothers, as he himself had. Perhaps this was only a way of expressing the childish idea that everything has its name, primordial and unchangeable. A nameless thing may well seem to a child no less of a contradiction than a thing without any size. Perhaps, too, the name as an external sound joins itself to and qualifies the thing in a way that we, who are wont to employ words as our own created signs, can hardly enter into.

A second direction of this early questioning is toward the reason and the cause of things. The typical form is 'why?' . . . Who that has tried to instruct the small child of three or four does not know the long, shrill, whine-like sound of this question? This form of question develops naturally out of the earlier, for to give the 'what' of a thing – that is, its connections – is to give its 'why' – that is, its mode of production, its use and purpose' . . .

Nothing is more interesting to a child than the production of things. What hours and hours does he not spend in wondering how the pebbles, the stones, the birds, the babies are made! This vivid interest in production is to a considerable extent practical. It is one of the great joys of children to be able themselves to make things, and the desire to fashion things which is probably at first quite immense, and befitting rather a god than a feeble child, naturally leads on to know something about the mode of producing. Yet from the earliest a true speculative interest blends with this practical instinct. Children are in the complete sense little philosophers, if philosophy, as the ancients said, consists in knowing the cause of things – *causas rerum cognoscere* . . .

The 'why' takes on a more special meaning when the idea of purpose and adaptation of means to ends

49

becomes clear. The search now is for the end, what philosophers call the teleological cause or reason. Here, again, the child sets out with the familiar type of experience, with human production and action as determined by aim. And it is easy for him, his mind being possessed by this anthropomorphic fancy which gives life to all things, to carry out this kind of inquiry. There is a stage in the development of a child's intelligence when questions such as 'Why do the leaves fall?' 'Why does the thunder make such a noise?' are answered most satisfactorily by a poetic fiction – by saying, for example, that the leaves are old and tired of hanging on to trees, and that the thunder-giant is in a particularly bad temper, and making a row. It is perhaps permissible to make use of this fiction at times, more especially perhaps when trying to answer the untiring questioning about animals and their doings – a region of existence, by the way, of which even the wisest of us knows exceedingly little. Yet the device has its risks; and an ill-considered piece of myth-making passed off as an answer may find itself awkwardly confronted by that most merciless of things, a child's logic . . .

Along with [a] tendency to push back inquiry to the unreachable beginning of things we mark a more modest and scientific line of investigation into the observable and explainable processes of Nature. Some questions which a busy listener would pooh-pooh as dreamy have a genuinely scientific value, showing that the little inquirer is trying to work out some problem of fact. This is illustrated by a question put by a little boy aged three years and nine months. 'Why don't we see two things with our two eyes?' a problem which, as we know, has exercised older psychologists . . .

If now and then they torment their elders with a string of random, reckless questionings, in how many cases, one wonders, are they not made to suffer – and that wrongfully – by having perfectly serious questions rudely cast back on their hands? The truth is, that to understand and to answer children's questions is a considerable art, including a large and deep knowledge of things, and a quick, sympathetic insight into the little questioners' minds.

MARIA MONTESSORI, MD

– *from* Dr Montessori's Own Handbook (1914) –

The Italian educator Maria Montessori, MD (1870–1952) opened her first *Casa dei Bambini* in Rome in 1906. There, she took what she had learned from her research with children with cognitive delays and disabilities to develop her approach to early education. She had seen that if you gave children a choice between toys and child-sized tools of everyday life – things like brooms, hammers and pots and pans – they would choose the tools, and adopt a self-disciplined regime of learning, by using them through play.

At the time *Dr Montessori's Own Handbook* was published in 1914, she had attained international fame, with Montessori methods adopted in schools from Argentina and the US, to the UK and Sweden, to Japan and Australia. Today, there are about 20,000 Montessori schools around the world.

R ecent years have seen a remarkable improvement in the conditions of child life. In all civilized countries, but especially in England, statistics show a decrease in infant mortality . . .

[A] corresponding improvement is to be seen in the physical development of children; they are physically finer and more vigorous. It has been the diffusion, the popularization of science, which has brought about such notable advantages. Mothers have learned to welcome the dictates of modern hygiene and to put them into practice in bringing up their children. Many new social institutions have sprung up and have been perfected with the object of assisting children and protecting them during the period of physical growth . . .

What has science done to effect this? Science has suggested for us certain very simple rules by which the child has been restored as nearly as possible to conditions of a natural life, and an order and a guiding law have been given to the functions of the body. For example, it is science which suggested maternal feeding, the abolition of swaddling clothes, baths, life in the open air, exercise, simple short clothing, quiet and plenty of sleep . . .

Yet with all this, science made no contribution that was entirely new. Mothers had always nursed their children, children had always been clothed, they had breathed and eaten before. The point is, that the same physical acts which, performed blindly and without order, led to disease and death, when ordered *rationally* were the means of giving strength and life . . .

Children must grow not only in the body but in the spirit, and the mother longs to follow the mysterious spiritual journey of the beloved one who tomorrow will be the intelligent, divine creation, man . . .

Motor Education. The education of the movements is very complex, as it must correspond to all the coordinated movements which the child has to establish in his physiological organism. The child, if left without guidance, is disorderly in his movements, and these disorderly movements are the *special characteristics of the little child.* In fact, he 'never keeps still', and 'touches everything'. This is what forms the child's so-called 'unruliness' and 'naughtiness'.

The adult world would deal with him by checking these movements, with the monotonous and useless repetition 'keep still'. As a matter of fact, in these movements the little one is seeking the very exercise which will organize and coordinate the movements useful to man. We must, therefore, desist from the useless attempt to reduce the child to a state of immobility. We should rather give 'order' to his movements, leading them to those actions towards which his efforts are actually tending . . . Once a direction is given to them, the child's movements are made towards a definite end, so that he himself grows quiet and contented, and becomes an active worker, a being calm and full of joy . . .

Freedom. It is necessary for the teacher to *guide* the child without letting him feel her presence too much, so that she may be always ready to supply the desired help, but may never be the obstacle between the child and his experience.

A lesson in the ordinary use of the word cools the child's enthusiasm for the knowledge of things, just as it would cool the enthusiasm of adults. To keep alive that enthusiasm is the secret of real guidance, and it will not prove a difficult task, provided that the attitude towards the child's acts be that of respect, calm and waiting, and provided that he be left free in his movements and in his experiences.

Then we shall notice that the child has a personality which he is seeking to expand; he has initiative, he chooses his own work, persists in it, changes it according to his inner needs; he does not shirk effort, he rather goes in search of it, and with great joy overcomes obstacles within his capacity. He is sociable to the extent of wanting to share with everyone his successes, his discoveries, and his little triumphs. There is therefore no need of intervention. 'Wait while observing.' That is the motto for the educator.

Let us wait, and be always ready to share in both the joys and the difficulties which the child experiences. He himself invites our sympathy, and we should respond fully and gladly. Let us have endless patience with his slow progress, and show enthusiasm and gladness at his successes. If we could say: 'We are respectful and courteous in our dealings with children, we treat them as we should like to be treated ourselves,' we should certainly have mastered a great educational principle and undoubtedly be setting an *example of good education*.

What we all desire for ourselves, namely, not to be disturbed in our work, not to find hindrances to our efforts, to have good friends ready to help us in times of need, to see them rejoice with us, to be on terms of equality with them, to be able to confide and trust in them – this is what we need for happy companionship. In the same way children are human beings to whom respect is due, superior to us by reason of their 'innocence' and of the greater possibilities of their future. What we desire they desire also.

As a rule, however, we do not respect our children. We try to force them to follow us without regard to their special needs. We are overbearing with them, and above all, rude; and then we expect them to be submissive and well-behaved, knowing all the time how strong is their instinct of imitation and how touching their faith in and admiration of us. They will imitate us in any case. Let us treat them, therefore, with all the kindness which we would wish to help to develop in them. And by kindness is not meant caresses . . . Kindness consists in interpreting the wishes of others, in conforming one's self to them, and sacrificing, if need be, one's own desire. This is the kindness which we must show towards children.

JOHN B. WATSON with ROSALIE RAYNER

– *from* Conditioned Emotional Reactions (1920) –

The married American psychologists John B. Watson (1878–1958) and Rosalie Rayner (1898–1935) conducted their first experiments with 'Little Albert' in 1919. They had recruited the boy with the aim of seeing if they could train him to fear something which he was not afraid of. After allowing him to play peacefully with a gentle lab rat, they made a loud sound, startling the infant into sobs. They did this again. The third time, 'Little Albert' began to cry as soon as he saw his previous pet. Over time, he began to cry whenever something furry was brought to him – a bunny, or a bearded Santa Claus mask – anticipating the distressing *CLACK*.

The Watsons' work inspired a researcher called Mary Cover Jones to conduct a mirror experiment, in which she conditioned a child with a phobia of furry objects to no longer fear them. She did this by exposing the boy, 'Peter', to a rabbit while he was in a group of other children lacking any fear of it.

Of course, under today's ethics codes, neither experiment would be allowed.

I n infancy the original emotional reaction patterns are few, consisting so far as observed of fear, rage and love . . . The early home life of the child furnishes a laboratory situation for establishing conditioned emotional responses. The present authors have recently put the whole matter to an experimental test.

Experimental work had been done so far on only one child, Albert B. This infant was reared almost from birth in a hospital environment; his mother was a wet nurse in the Harriet Lane Home for Invalid Children. Albert's life was normal: he was healthy from birth and one of the best developed youngsters ever brought to the hospital, weighing twenty-one pounds at nine months of age. He was on the whole stolid and unemotional. His stability was one of the principal reasons for using him as a subject in this test. We felt that we could do him relatively little harm by carrying out such experiments as those outlined below.

At approximately nine months of age we ran him through the emotional tests that have become a part of our regular routine in determining whether fear reactions can be called out by other stimuli than sharp noises and the sudden removal of support . . . In brief, the infant was confronted suddenly and for the first time successively with a white rat, a rabbit, a dog, a monkey, with masks with and without hair, cotton wool, burning newspapers, etc. A permanent record of Albert's reactions to these objects and situations has been preserved in a motion picture study. Manipulation was the most usual reaction called out. At no time did this infant ever show fear in any situation. These experimental records were confirmed by the casual observations of the mother and hospital attendants. No one had ever seen him in a state of fear and rage. The infant practically never cried.

Up to approximately nine months of age we had not tested him with loud sounds. The test to determine whether a fear reaction could be called out by a loud sound was made when he was eight months, twenty-six days of age. The sound was that made by striking a hammer upon a suspended steel bar four feet in length and three-fourths of an inch in diameter. The laboratory notes are as follows:

One of the two experimenters caused the child to turn its head and fixate her moving hand; the other stationed back of the child, struck the steel bar a sharp blow. The child started violently, his breathing was checked and the arms were raised in a characteristic manner. On the second stimulation the same thing occurred, and in addition the lips began to pucker and tremble. On the third stimulation the child broke into a sudden crying fit. This is the first time an emotional situation in the laboratory has produced any fear or even crying in Albert.

We had expected just these results on account of our work with other infants brought up under similar conditions. It is worth while to call attention to the fact that removal of support (dropping and jerking the blanket upon which the infant was lying) was tried exhaustively upon this infant on the same occasion. It was not effective in producing the fear response. This stimulus is effective in younger children. At what age such stimuli lose their potency in producing fear is not known. Nor is it known whether less placid children ever lose their fear of them. This probably depends upon the training the child gets. It is well known that children eagerly run to be tossed into the air and caught. On the other hand it is equally well known that in the adult fear responses are called out quite clearly by the sudden removal of support, if the individual is walking across a bridge, walking out upon a beam, etc.

THE PROGRESSIVE GROCER

– Our Advice to Mothers (1924) –

In the early twentieth century, parenting advice became fixated on the need to expose young, growing children to plentiful fresh air, preferably outdoors. This came at a time when more and more families were leaving rural districts to live in urban tenements. A year before this recipe for children's health and happiness was published in a New Jersey newspaper, a mother and inventor called Emma Read received US patent no. 1,448,235 for a 'portable baby cage' that could be safely hung off a window ledge. 'This construction of cage will be very useful in cities where the houses are very close together and in apartments, where there are no front and back yards or lawns, for the babies and children to play on,' she said in her patent application.

If you want to preserve children, follow these directions. Take:

One large grassy field

One half-dozen children

Two or three small dogs

A pinch of brook and pebbles

Mix children and dogs well together and put them in a field, stirring constantly. Pour brook over pebbles; sprinkle field with flowers; spread over all a deep blue sky; and bake in the sun. When brown, remove, and set to cool in a bath tub.

BERTRAND RUSSELL

– *from* On Education, Especially in Early Childhood (1926) –

As a philosopher, Bertrand Russell (1872–1970) was celebrated as a logician. As a British public intellectual, he was an outspoken anti-imperialist and pacifist who championed freedom of expression and cooperation. After his first son was born in 1921, he grew interested in how the competing fields of psychoanalysis and behaviourism might inform his parenting.

Logically, he believed it was essential to take a 'properly scientific outlook' – for instance, observing that children ask the same question again and again not because they have forgotten the answer but because they are trying to see if the answer stays the same. He believed the parent's paramount job is to create a sense of safety and consistency, then give the child freedom to develop: 'A child needs to grow like a tree, quietly, in one spot, at his own pace and in his own manner.'

T he new-born infant has reflexes and instincts, but no habits . . . There is one well-developed instinct, the instinct of sucking; when the child is engaged in this occupation, it feels at home with its new environment. But the rest of its waking life is passed in a vague bewilderment, from which relief is found by sleeping most of the twenty-four hours. At the end of a fortnight, all this is changed. The child has acquired expectations from regularly recurring experiences. It is already a conservative – probably a more complete conservative than at any later time. Any novelty is met with resentment. If it could speak, it would say: 'Do you suppose I am going to change the habits of a lifetime at my time of life?' The rapidity with which infants acquire habits is amazing. Every bad habit acquired is a barrier to better habits later; that is why the first formation of habits in early infancy is so important. If the first habits are good, endless trouble is saved later. Moreover, habits acquired very early feel, in later life, just like instincts; they have the same profound grip . . .

Two considerations come in when we are considering habit-formation in infancy. The first and paramount consideration is health; the second is character. We want the child to become the sort of person that will be liked and will be able to cope with life successfully. Fortunately, health and character point in the same direction: what is good for one is good also for the other. It is character that specially concerns us in this book; but health requires the same practices. Thus we are not faced with the difficult alternative of a healthy scoundrel or a diseased saint.

Every educated mother now-a-days knows such simple facts as the importance of feeding the infant at regular intervals, not whenever it cries. This practice has arisen because it is better for the child's digestion, which is an entirely sufficient reason. But it is also desirable from the point of view of moral education. Infants are far more cunning (not in the American sense) than grown-up people are apt to suppose; if they find that crying produces agreeable results, they will cry. When, in later life, a habit of complaining causes them to be disliked instead of petted, they feel surprised and resentful, and the world seems to them cold and unsympathetic. If, however, they grow up into charming women, they will still be petted when they are querulous, and the bad training begun in childhood will be intensified. The same thing is true of rich men. Unless the right methods are adopted in infancy, people in later life will be either discontented or grasping, according to the degree of their power. The right moment to begin the requisite moral training is the moment of birth, because then it can be begun without disappointing expectations. At any later time, it will have to fight against contrary habits, and will consequently be met by resentful indignation.

In dealing with the infant, therefore, there is need of a delicate balance between neglect and indulgence. Everything necessary for health must be done. The child must be picked up when it suffers from wind, it must be kept dry and warm. But if it cries when there is no adequate physical cause, it must be left to cry; if not, it will quickly develop into a tyrant . . . At no period of its life must it be regarded as an agreeable pet, somewhat more interesting than a lap-dog. It must from the very first be viewed seriously, as a potential adult. Habits which would be intolerable in an adult may be quite pleasant in a child. Of course the child cannot actually have the habits of an adult, but we should avoid everything that places an obstacle in the way of the acquisition of these habits . . .

As soon as the child can focus, it finds pleasure in watching moving objects, especially things that wave in the wind. But the number of possible amusements is small, until the child has learned to grasp objects that it sees. Then, immediately, there is an enormous accession of pleasure. For some time, the exercise of grasping is enough to secure the happiness of many waking hours. Pleasure in a rattle also comes at this stage. Slightly earlier is the conquest of the toes and fingers. At first, the movement of the toes is purely reflex; then the baby discovers that they can be moved at will. This gives all the pleasure of an imperialist conquering a foreign country: the toes cease to be alien bodies and become incorporated in the ego. From this time onward, the child should be able to find many amusements, provided suitable objects are within his reach. And a child's amusements, for the most part, will be just what its education requires – provided, of course, that it is not allowed to tumble, or to swallow pins, or otherwise injure itself.

The first three months of life are, on the whole, a somewhat dreary time for the infant, except during the moments when it is enjoying its meals. When it is comfortable, it sleeps; when it is awake, there is usually some discomfort. The happiness of a human being depends upon mental capacities, but these can find little outlet in an infant under three months, for lack of experience and muscular control. Young animals enjoy life much sooner, because they depend more upon instinct and less upon experience; but the things an infant can do by instinct are too few to provide more than a minimum of pleasure and interest. On the whole, the first three months involve a good deal of boredom. But boredom is necessary if there is to be enough sleep; if much is done to amuse the child, it will not sleep enough.

At about the age of two to three months, the child learns to smile, and to have feelings about persons which are different from its feelings about things. At this age a social relation between mother and child begins to be possible: the child can and does show pleasure at the sight of the mother, and develops responses which are not merely animal. Very soon a desire for praise and approval grows up; in my own boy, it was first shown unmistakably at the age of five months, when he succeeded, after many attempts, in lifting a somewhat heavy bell off the table, and ringing it while he looked round at everybody with a proud smile. From this moment, the educator has a new weapon: praise and blame. This weapon is extraordinarily powerful throughout childhood, but it must be used with great caution. There should not be any blame at all during the first year, and afterwards it should be used very sparingly. Praise is less harmful. But it should not be given so easily as to lose its value, nor should it be used to over-stimulate a child. No tolerable parent could refrain from praising a child when it first walks and when it first says an intelligible word. And generally, when a child has mastered a difficulty after persistent efforts, praise is a proper reward. Moreover, it is well to let the child feel that you sympathize with his desire to learn.

But on the whole an infant's desire to learn is so strong that parents need only provide opportunity. Give the child a chance to develop, and his own efforts will do the rest. It is not necessary to teach a child to crawl, or to walk, or to learn any of the other elements of muscular control. Of course we teach a child to talk by talking to it, but I doubt whether any purpose is served by deliberate attempts to teach words. Children learn at their own pace, and it is a mistake to try to force them. The great incentive to effort, all through life, is experience of success after initial difficulties. The difficulties must not be so great as to cause discouragement, or so small as not to stimulate effort. From birth to death, this is a fundamental principle. It is by what we do ourselves that we learn. What grown-up people can do is to perform some simple action that the child would like to perform, such as rattling a rattle, and then let the child find out how to do it. What others do is merely a stimulus to ambition; it is never in itself an education.

Regularity and routine are of the utmost importance in early childhood, and most of all in the first year of life. In regard to sleep, food, and evacuation, regular habits should be formed from the start. Moreover, familiarity of surroundings is very important mentally. It teaches recognition, it avoids overstrain, and it produces a feeling of safety. I have sometimes thought that belief in the uniformity of nature, which is said to be a postulate of science, is entirely derived from the wish for safety. We can cope with the expected, but if the laws of nature were suddenly changed we should perish. The infant, because of its weakness, has need of reassurance, and it will be happier if everything that happens seems to happen according to invariable laws, so as to be predictable. In later childhood, the love of adventure develops, but in the first year of life everything unusual tends to be alarming . . . It learns more in the first twelve months than it will ever learn again in the same space of time, and this would be impossible if it had not a very active intelligence.

To sum up: Treat even the youngest baby with respect, as a person who will have to take his place in the world. Do not sacrifice his future to your present convenience, or to your pleasure in making much of him: the one is as harmful as the other. Here, as elsewhere, a combination of love and knowledge is necessary if the right way is to be followed.

MARGARET MEAD

– *from* The Education of the Samoan Child (1928) –

Coming of Age in Samoa, the seminal work of the anthropologist Margaret Mead (1901–1978) is primarily interested in teenagers' lives and sexual awakenings. However, in her first chapter, on 'The Education of the Samoan Child', she commented on early psychosocial development, such as the household and childcaring responsibilities given to children at a young age. Later anthropologists, such as Barbara Rogoff, would call this 'Learning by Observing and Pitching In', and document its prevalence in a wide range of cultures, including among families living in modern cities.

During her fieldwork, Mead noted that breastfeeding was done whenever the child was hungry, rather than on a schedule. Her observations of parenting in so-called traditional societies were said to have influenced the thinking of her own children's paediatrician – one Dr Benjamin Spock.

From birth until the age of four or five, a child's education is exceedingly simple. They must be house-broken, a matter made more difficult by an habitual indifference to the activities of very small children. They must learn to sit or crawl within the house and never to stand upright unless it is absolutely necessary; never to address an adult in a standing position; to stay out of the sun; not to tangle the strands of the weaver; not to scatter the cut-up cocoanut which is spread out to dry; to keep their scant loin cloths at least nominally fastened to their persons; to treat fire and knives with proper caution; not to touch the kava bowl, or the kava cup; and, if their father is a chief, not to crawl on his bed-place when he is by. These are really simply a series of avoidances, enforced by occasional cuffings and a deal of exasperated shouting and ineffectual conversation.

The weight of the punishment usually falls upon the next oldest child, who learns to shout, 'Come out of the sun,' before she has fully appreciated the necessity of doing so herself. By the time Samoan girls and boys have reached sixteen or seventeen years of age these perpetual admonitions to the younger ones have become an inseparable part of their conversation, a monotonous, irritated undercurrent to all their comments. I have known them to intersperse their remarks every two or three minutes with, 'Keep still,' 'Sit still,' 'Keep your mouths shut,' 'Stop that noise,' uttered quite mechanically although all of the little ones present may have been behaving as quietly as a row of intimidated mice. On the whole, this last requirement of silence is continually mentioned and never enforced. The little nurses are more interested in peace than in forming the characters of their small charges and when

71

a child begins to howl, it is simply dragged out of earshot of its elders. No mother will ever exert herself to discipline a younger child if an older one can be made responsible.

If small families of parents and children prevailed in Samoa, this system would result in making half of the population solicitous and self-sacrificing and the other half tyrannous and self-indulgent. But just as a child is getting old enough so that its wilfulness is becoming unbearable, a younger one is saddled upon it, and the whole process is repeated again, each child being disciplined and socialised through responsibility for a still younger one.

CLEON C. MASON, MD

– *from* Child-Pestering Parents (1930) –

It took less than a generation to stir up a backlash against the doctrine of psychoanalysis put forward by Freud, who imagined children's development as a series of psychosexual conflicts and neuroses such as 'mother fixation'. Equally in the sights of critics were behaviourists like the Watsons, who believed children, like any animal young, could be trained to do anything. But there was another group of child specialists increasingly telling parents what to do: companies selling products in the age of advertising.

A piece published in the *North American Review* argued that this cacophony of so-called experts was 'making little hypochondriacs of our youngsters'.

They were three fine boys; sturdy little tykes who ate well, slept well and grew normally. They did the customary amount of fighting, collected the usual assortment of diseases, warts, freckles and broken bones, ran away on occasions, learned their lessons under protest, devilled the neighborhood cats and dogs, kidded the cop – wholesomely dirty, disgustingly healthy . . .

For no sane reason their mother suddenly developed a serious attack of child study. She haunted the library, she devoured unbelievable quantities of literature on child psychology; complexes of every known variety became her mental diet; she stuffed herself with strange ideas to a point of intellectual indigestion. No distance was too great to travel if she could hear a new lecture on the subject of children. Each boy was charted and cross-indexed; every activity, normal and dear to the hearts of little fellows, was duly plotted. That affair of the pup and the tin can became as horrible as Banquo's ghost, as significant as a visitation from the Almighty; healthy sex curiosity became a leering nightmare. In the end the mother made herself exceedingly unhappy, made her husband willing to stay at the club until all hours, and developed a shy apprehensiveness in her children.

Finally, she consulted the old family doctor, who laughed rather irreverently at her new deity. He was promptly discharged!

At a bridge party she heard many Ohs and Ahs over the city's newest child specialist, and hastened to consult him. He was all sympathy, all helpfulness. He gave her books of which she had heard only in a misty way. He talked long and learnedly of repressions, sublimations, IQ's, inferiority complexes and a host of abstruse psychological conceptions which have no business in such a place. He examined the awed boys endlessly, he criticised their diet – hot dogs and hamburgers became monstrous; a good healthy sweat indicated a trip to the undertaker; and as to lollypops, fighting and pet guinea pigs, heaven forbid! He stripped them of their priceless overalls and substituted neat knickers, blouses and neckties – for their self-respect, you know! He made a surreptitious swim an impossibility by forcing 'Childwarm' underwear upon them. He predicted flat feet and a life of aches and pains unless 'True-Foot' shoes were promptly donned. In the end I am not sure who suffered most, the mother who grew more befuddled every day, the father who shelled out a lot of money needlessly, or the three boys bereft of every natural impulse who became neurasthenic little Lord Fauntleroys. One can only weep with Lear:

> Poor naked wretches wheresoe'er you are
> Who bide the pelting of this pitiless storm.

These are three real boys. They . . . are in for a lot of trouble unless someone can get their mother to give up the dangerous mental liquor she is tippling. The stuff is intoxicating, and especially devastating when it falls into the hands of persons, medically trained or otherwise, who have not the common sense to use it judiciously.

If this were an isolated case one would not worry, and though it is far from what normally happens it occurs often enough to cause alarm.

We are making altogether too much fuss over our children. Ignorant sentimentalists have orated; well meaning but misguided students have written;

the doctor has added fuel to the fire, often unwittingly lest he be found wanting. All in all a system of child worship has been reared on the flimsy foundation of foolish sentimentality, and so unstable is the structure that one cannot help wondering when it will topple and in the end destroy the object of its tender solicitude.

Two outstanding factors have contributed to the situation. As a nation we have moved from the country to the city. This left the child with no place to go but the streets and nothing to do in the way of regular chores. Formerly he played around the farm, learned to milk the cows, feed the stock and help in many ways. It never occurred to parents or to teachers that the child had been wrenched from a wholly natural atmosphere to one charged with artificiality and danger, from a life where day after day he performed the duties which fell to his lot, played serenely with whatever came to hand while his father tilled the soil and his mother busied herself with household duties, both too busy providing food and shelter to waste much time delving into the business of the children. He needed some substitute, and when his self-developed substitutions took on a shocking complexion his elders were duly horrified. Most parents and teachers explained it satisfactorily as pure cussedness; a few preachers shouted original sin; the youngsters came in for a fair share of berating, lingual and manual, but no marked improvement took place until sufficient athletics and shop work were introduced into the school to offset partly the persistent idleness. Then came Freud! . . .

Children have been spied upon by hordes. The doctor, the merciless school-psychologist, social workers and parents have pried into the lives of the little folks until every vestige of privacy has been stripped away. I am speaking kindly. I do not question the sincerity of these well-meaning people, but I do question most seriously whether the good they have accomplished in a better understanding of the child or in improved methods of training has in any way repaid us for the damage done.

Fortunately the child has a clearer outlook and a keener mind than his adult benefactors, otherwise he would have succumbed long ago. Most children have the happy faculty of going serenely along their own inscrutable and I believe immutable ways, conscious no doubt that they are being spied upon but rather contemptuously accepting it as just another minor nuisance such as whooping cough, baths or Sunday School. The perspicacity of the average child is mighty armor.

Were the onslaughts of pseudo-psychologists, driving teachers, ultra-scientific doctors and misguided parents the only enemies of normal childhood, the younger generation would have more than an even break; but the infant is beset from the first lusty howl!

Birth records are public property. Within a week after the registration of a birth the proud parents are deluged with literature ranging in character from the latest food fad to the most recent development in safety pins. Commercial firms tirelessly disguise advertising in pretty pink and blue booklets, describing patent foods which put plebeian breast milk to shame, clothing without which no child can expect to avoid terrible diseases, and numerous other articles which any self-respecting infant really needs; and the worst of it is, every article extolled has a world of medical recommendations. The parents, new at the business, read every word; they find a mass of contradictory statements, and ere long are hopelessly muddled. Their anxiety that the bawling future President be saved for his country is intensified by the sly innuendoes of these commercial pests – suppose they should make a mistake – suppose 'Grandma's Soup' *is* better than breast milk – from such simple beginnings grows a type of unholy watchfulness, a watchfulness so nearly hysterical in its pervasion that it reflects very seriously on the natural development of the sensitive child . . .

Part of this unhealthy state of affairs is directly traceable to the doctor, especially the child specialist. It would seem that the aim of doctors limiting their work to children should be to teach parents how to raise a healthy child with the least expenditure of energy and cash. After reading page upon page of printed instructions which some mothers receive, one wonders. The fearful and final tone leaves the parents in a poor state of mind to go forward with any common sense régime . . .

A child is born with certain inalienable rights, such as measles, runny nose, broken bones, warts, fighting, dirt, green apples and tummy aches. Yet we would deprive him of all these! We would hothouse him day in and day out, mother him to death, pester him with all sorts of foolish notions of which the pesterers are as ignorant as the child. I for one am glad I was born before psychology became a fad and Freud a best seller . . .

The keynote of child raising is the old byword of statecraft – *laissez-faire*! A child as well as an adult is entitled to privacy, has a right to learn for himself, loves mothering but vigorously protests smothering. He will thrive on well-directed inattention; he will wither, grow cross, irritable and defiant when made the victim of persistent Paul Prys . . .

Remember always that your child has many lessons to learn and that he can learn these only by independent action, independent thinking, and free investigation of the complex world around him. Most children are adept at minding their own business: would we could say the same for adults!

ERIK H. ERIKSON

– *from* Eight Ages of Man (1950) –

Erik Erikson (1902–1994) formulated one of the twentieth century's most influential theories of psychosocial development. In it, he identified eight life stages, each with one primary tension which will mould personal identity and relationships. Life in infancy is dominated by the development of either trust or mistrust. In early childhood, life is focused on becoming physically autonomous – or, when this fails, feeling doubt. With preschool comes a tension between taking initiative and feelings of guilt; at school age, between industriousness and feelings of inferiority. And so life proceeds, through adolescence, young adulthood, middle adulthood and the later years of maturity.

In Erikson's view, development is not merely biological. It is shaped by the people around us – most especially, in the early stages of life, by a child's relationship with their parents.

Basic Trust vs. Basic Mistrust

The first demonstration of social trust in the baby is the ease of his feeding, the depth of his sleep, the relaxation of his bowels. The experience of a mutual regulation of his increasingly receptive capacities with the maternal techniques of provision gradually helps him to balance the discomfort caused by the immaturity of homeostasis with which he was born. In his gradually increasing waking hours he finds that more and more adventures of the senses arouse a feeling of familiarity, of having coincided with a feeling of inner goodness. Forms of comfort, and people associated with them, become as familiar as the gnawing discomfort of the bowels. The infant's first social achievement, then, is his willingness to let the mother out of sight without undue anxiety or rage, because she has become an inner certainty as well as an outer predictability. ...

Mothers create a sense of trust in their children by that kind of administration which in its quality combines sensitive care of the baby's individual needs and a firm sense of personal trustworthiness within the trusted framework of their culture's life style. This forms the basis in the child for a sense of identity which will later combine a sense of being 'all right', of being oneself, and of becoming what other people trust one will become. There are, therefore (within certain limits . . . defined as the 'musts' of child care), few frustrations in either this or the following stages which the growing child cannot endure if the frustration leads to the every-renewed experience of greater sameness and stronger continuity of development, toward a final integration of the individual life cycle with some meaningful wider belongingness. Parents must not only have certain ways of guiding by prohibition and permission; they must also be able to represent to the child a deep, an almost somatic conviction that there is a meaning to what they are doing . . .

Autonomy vs. Shame and Doubt

In describing the growth and crises of the human person as a series of alternative basic attitudes such as trust vs. mistrust, we take recourse to the term a 'sense of', although, like a 'sense of health', or a 'sense of being unwell', such 'senses' pervade surface and depth, consciousness and the unconscious. They are, then, at the same time, ways of *experiencing* accessible to introspection; ways of *behaving*, observable by others; and unconscious *inner states* determinable by test and analysis. It is important to keep these three dimensions in mind . . .

Muscular maturation sets the stage for experimentation with two simultaneous sets of social modalities: holding on and letting go. As is the case with all of these modalities, their basic conflicts can lead in the end to either hostile or benign expectations and attitudes. Thus, to hold can become a destructive and cruel retaining or restraining, and it can become a pattern of care: to have and to hold. To let go, too, can turn into an inimical letting loose of destructive forces, or it can become a relaxed 'to let pass' and 'to let be'.

Outer control at this stage, therefore, must be

firmly reassuring. The infant must come to feel that the basic faith in existence, which is the lasting treasure saved from the rages of [infancy], will not be jeopardized by this about-face of his, this sudden violent wish to have a choice, to appropriate demandingly, and to eliminate stubbornly. Firmness must protect him against the potential anarchy of his as yet untrained sense of discrimination, his inability to hold on and to let go with discretion. As his environment encourages him to 'stand on his own feet', it must protect him against meaningless and arbitrary experiences of shame and of early doubt . . .

Shame supposes that one is completely exposed and conscious of being looked at: in one word, self-conscious. One is visible and not ready to be visible; which is why we dream of shame as a situation in which we are stared at in a condition of incomplete dress, in night attire, 'with one's pants down'. . . .

Too much shaming does not lead to genuine propriety but to a secret determination to try to get away with things, unseen – if, indeed, it does not result in defiant shamelessness. There is an impressive American ballad in which a murderer to be hanged on the gallows before the eyes of the community, instead of feeling duly chastened, begins to berate the onlookers, ending every salvo of defiance with the words, 'God damn your eyes.' Many a small child, shamed beyond endurance, may be in a chronic mood (although not in possession of either the courage or the words) to express defiance in similar terms. What I mean by this sinister reference is that there is a limit to a child's and an adult's endurance in the face of demands to consider himself, his body, and his wishes as evil and dirty, and to his belief in the infallibility of those who pass such judgment. He may be apt to turn things around, and to consider as evil only the fact that they exist: his chance will come when they are gone, or when he will go from them.

Doubt is the brother of shame. Where shame is dependent on the consciousness of being upright and exposed, doubt, so clinical observation leads me to believe, has much to do with a consciousness of having a front and a back – and especially a 'behind' . . . [a] basic sense of doubt in whatever one has left behind . . .

Initiative vs. Guilt

There is in every child at every stage a new miracle of vigorous unfolding, which constitutes a new hope and a new responsibility for all. Such is the sense and the pervading quality of initiative. The criteria for all these sense and qualities are the same: a crisis, more or less beset with fumbling and fear, is resolved, in that the child suddenly seems to 'grow together' both in his person and in his body. He appears 'more himself', more loving, relaxed and brighter in his judgment, more activated and activating. He is in free possession of a surplus of energy which permits him to forget failures quickly and to approach what seems desirable (even if it also seems uncertain and even dangerous) with undiminished and more accurate direction. Initiative adds to autonomy the quality of undertaking, planning and 'attacking' a task for the sake of being active and on the move, where before self-will, more often than not, inspired acts of defiance or, at any rate, protested independence.

I know that the very word 'initiative' to many, has an American, and industrial connotation. Yet, initiative is a necessary part of every act, and man needs a sense of initiative for whatever he learns and does, from fruit-gathering to a system of enterprise.

The [toddler] ambulatory stage and that of infantile genitality add to the inventory of basic social modalities that of 'making', first in the sense of 'being on the make'. There is no simpler, stronger word for it; it suggests pleasure in attack and conquest . . .

The danger of this stage is a sense of guilt over the goals contemplated and the acts initiated in one's exuberant enjoyment of new locomotor and mental power: acts of aggressive manipulation and coercion which soon go far beyond the executive capacity of organism and mind and therefore call for an energetic halt on one's contemplated initiative . . . The child indulges in fantasies of being a giant and a tiger, but in his dreams he runs in terror for dear life . . .

The problem, again, is one of mutual regulation. Where the child, now so ready to overmanipulate himself, can gradually develop a sense of moral responsibility, where he can gain some insight into the institutions, functions, and roles which will permit his responsible participation, he will find pleasurable accomplishment in wielding tools and weapons, in manipulating meaningful toys – and in caring for younger children.

The child is at no time more ready to learn quickly and avidly, to become bigger in the sense of sharing obligation and performance than during this period of his development. He is eager and able to make things cooperatively, to combine with other children for the purpose of constructing and planning, and he is willing to profit from teachers and to emulate ideal prototypes . . . Social institutions, therefore, offer children of this age an *economic ethos*, in the form of ideal adults recognizable by their uniforms and their functions, and fascinating enough to replace, the heroes of picture book and fairy tale.

JEAN PIAGET

– *from* The Attainment of Invariants and Reversible Operations in the Development of Thinking (1953) –

Swiss psychologist Jean Piaget (1896–1980) revolution-ised the study of children's development.

In this lecture, Piaget provided an overview of three decades of research into how children think – the internal cognitive processes that are difficult to surface because children are still forming their understanding of the world. Through hundreds of novel experiments he identified four stages in the development of children's intelligence: the pre-language stage from birth to about age two; the pre-operational stage from about ages two to seven; the concrete operational stage from about ages seven to twelve; and the propositional stage of pre-ado-lescence and adolescence.

Here, he considers the first stages, as the child begins to understand that objects continue to exist even when they're outside view and then to grasp equivalence between groups of numbers, spaces and distances, cre-ating the base of knowledge for arithmetic and logic as they get older.

I nitially we relied exclusively on interviews and asked the children only verbal questions. This may have been a beginning, and it can yield certain types of results but, assuredly, it is not exhaustive.

Of late, our investigations have been conducted quite differently. We now try to start with some action that the child must perform. We introduce him into an experimental setting, present him with objects and – after the problem has been stated – the child must do something, he must experiment. Having observed his actions and manipulation of objects we can then pose the verbal questions that constitute the interview . . .

Furthermore, while our earlier studies pertained to various classes of thought content, we later became increasingly more interested in the formal aspects of thought. These aspects transcend any single content category and provide the basis for the intellectual elaboration of any and all contents . . . Our essential preoccupation has been the analysis of those complex structures of thought that seem to characterize the various developmental stages . . . I shall emphasize primarily one aspect of these structures, namely their reversibility. I use the term reversibility in its logical or mathematical sense, not in its physiological or medical connotation. I believe intelligence is above all characterized by the coordination of operations that are reversible actions.

Basically, to solve a problem is to coordinate operations while focusing on the solution. An operation is, first of all, an action. We shall see that at its inception intelligence begins with simple actions on the sensori-motor level, actions which then become interiorized and come to be represented symbolically. Moreover, operations are basically actions which can be performed in either direction, that is, actions which are reversible. This is really the remarkable thing about intelligence, if one compares intelligence with other mental functions, for instance habits. Habits are not reversible, they are oriented in one direction only. Thus, we have learned to write from left to right, and if we wanted to write from right to left we could not do so on the basis of our previous habits, we would have to start learning a new habit. By contrast, once we can handle an operation, for instance the operation of adding in the arithmetical sense, or in its more general logical sense, we can reverse that specific action. From the moment when the child understands what it means to add, that is, to bring together two groups to form one, he implicitly knows also what it means to separate the groups again, to dissociate them, to subtract . . . From the psychological point of view, one of the most fruitful terrains for the analysis of this reversibility is the problem of conservation.

In any system of reversible actions there results the construction of certain invariants, certain forms of conservation analogous to those subserving scientific reasoning. In the young child we can observe the development of these invariants . . . For instance, we can ask a child whether, when a given liquid is poured from a container A into another container

B of a different shape, the quantity of the liquid remains the same. For us that is self-evident, as it is for children above a certain age. But... for the younger children it is not self-evident at all. In fact, they will say the quantity has increased because the height of the new container is greater, or that it is less because container B is thinner. They have not yet attained the logically relevant concept of conservation and the pertinent invariants, and they cannot grasp these until some time later when their thinking becomes capable of reversible operations . . . Let us trace now, step by step, the development of this reversibility, of these forms of conservation . . .

The pre-language stage

At the present time everybody agrees that there is intelligent action prior to language. The baby demonstrates intelligent behavior before he can speak. Interestingly, we note, the earliest forms of intelligence already aim at the construction of certain invariants – practical invariants to be sure, namely invariants of the concrete space of immediate action. These first invariants are already the result of a sort of reversibility but it is a practical reversibility embedded in the very actions; it is not yet a constituent of thought proper. Of the invariants which arise at the sensori-motor stage perhaps the most important one is the scheme of the permanent object. I call the permanent object that object which continues to exist outside of the perceptual field . . . Such a scheme is not present from the very beginning. When, at about 4½ months of age, a child starts to reach for the things he sees in his visual field and, when he begins to coordinate vision and prehension to some extent, one can observe that he does not yet react to a permanent object. For instance, I may show the infant a watch, dangling it in front of him. He reaches out to take the watch, but at the very moment when he has already extended his hand, I cover the watch with a napkin. What happens? He promptly withdraws his hand as if the watch has been absorbed into the napkin. Even though he can very well remove the napkin if it is put over his own face, he does not lift it in order to look for the watch underneath. You might say that the watch is perhaps of no great interest to the infant; however, the same experiment can be made with a nursing bottle. I have done this with one of my children at the age of 7 months. At the time of his feeding I show him the bottle, he extends his hand to take it, but, at that moment, I hide it behind my arm. If he sees one end sticking out he kicks and screams and gives every indication of wanting to have it. If, however, the bottle is completely hidden and nothing sticks out, he stops crying and acts for all we know as if the bottle no longer existed, as if it had been dissolved and absorbed into my arm.

Towards the end of the first year the infant begins to search for the vanished object. Already at 9 or 10 months he looks for it behind a screen. If we place the child between two screens, for example, a cloth or a pillow on his right and another one at his left, we can make a very curious observation concerning the locus of the hiding place. With the child in that position I now show him, for instance, a watch. As soon as he evinces interest in the watch I place it under the cloth at his right. Thereupon the child will promptly lift the cloth and grasp the watch. Now I take it from him and, very slowly, so that he can follow with his eyes, move the watch over to his left side. Then, having made sure that he has indeed followed the movement, I cover the watch in its new position. I have observed this in my three children over varying periods of time, and we have repeated this experiment frequently since. There is a stage when, at the moment the child sees the watch disappear at the left, he immediately turns back to the right and looks for the watch there. In other words, he looks for the object where he has found it before. The object is not yet a mobile thing, capable of movements and correlated displacements . . .

Finally, towards the end of the first year the object comes to have a degree of independent existence. Its disappearance elicits search, and that search is guided by the observed displacements . . .

The pre-operational stage

Let us now turn to the development of representational thinking proper. We observe it first in play, in imaginary games with their fictitious qualities and symbolic aspects, play in which one thing comes to be represented by means of another thing. Differentiated imitation, for instance of various people in the child's environment, and a variety of other symbolic acts belong to this stage. Such representational thinking greatly enlarges the range of intellectual activity . . . This takes place in the period which extends from the beginning of language to the age of about seven or eight years at the other end. During this period we can already speak of thought, of representation, but not yet of logical operations defined as interiorized reversible action systems . . .

We can ask the child to put blue beads into container A and red beads into container B, and we make sure that each time he places a blue bead into container A he also places a red bead into the other container B, so that there will be the same number of beads in each of the two containers. The child is then told to pour the beads from container B into a new container, C; thereupon we ask him if there are the same number of beads in C as in A . . . Now a curious thing happens. Until approximately the age of 6½ years the child believes the number of beads has changed, that there are more beads in container

C because it is higher than B, or that there are fewer beads in container C because it is thinner than B. If you ask him 'Where do these extra beads come from?' or 'What happened to the beads that are no longer there?' he is very much surprised at your question. He is totally uninterested in the mechanism of the transformation. What interests him is the gross perceptual configuration which is different in the two situations; even in the case of these discrete entities there is no conservation of absolute quantities.

The same can be shown with respect to the correspondence of numbers. You can make the following experiment. The child is presented with an alignment of six blue poker chips, one next to the other, and is given a box of red poker chips with the request to construct a similar array with as many red poker chips as there are blue poker chips in the model . . . There is a primitive stage at approximately 4 to 4½ years when the child simply places chips in a line of similar length without regard for any one-to-one correspondence of the components. Thus, he defines quantity essentially in terms of occupied space. The second stage is much more interesting and lasts approximately to age 6½ to 7 years. Here we find exact correspondence between the number of chips in the model and those placed by the child. Many authors have been satisfied with this visual correspondence, and they have concluded that it is proof of the child's understanding of numbers. We can show, however, that this is not the case. All you have to do is to spread the chips of one of the two groups a little further apart, or to push them closer together, and the child will no longer think that the two alignments contain identical quantities . . .

Another example is the following: We confront the child with two identical green cardboards and tell him that these are two pastures where cows can graze. Both have lots of grass, so much, in fact, that if you put a cow half-way between the two she cannot decide which one to choose. At this point the child readily agrees that obviously the two pastures must be equal. Now the farmer who owns the first pasture puts up a house in one corner. The second farmer, who owns the other pasture, builds exactly the same kind of house but, instead of putting it in the corner he puts it right in the middle of the pasture. Do equal amounts of grass remain on the two pastures now? Already here the configuration is somewhat different but you see a good number of children who will tell you that it is the same on both pastures when there is only one house. Next the first farmer puts up another house adjoining the first one in the corner, and the second farmer puts another one here, adjoining the one in the middle. Are there still equal amounts of grass to be had from the two pastures? Starting with two houses it has become complicated. There are children who will tell us that there is lots more grass in the one pasture than in the other. Remember Euclid's theorem that if you take two equal quantities from two equal quantities there remain two equal quantities? That is the same logic that presupposes conservation, but here we have no conservation and Euclid's axiom is not yet valid for the 5-year-old.

HARRY F. HARLOW

– *from* The Nature of Love (1958) –

The research programme of American psychologist Harry Harlow (1905–1981) was controversial even in its own day. Who would devise an experiment that deprived a developing infant of its mother? Even where the infant was a rhesus macaque, the act felt inhumane.

Harlow had taken up the practice for logistical reasons. In the 1930s he had developed a test to study monkey cognition and observed that the monkeys appeared to learn. He wanted to understand how this skill developed, and in order to have many young monkeys for cognitive experiments, he needed to raise them in a lab. In the 1950s, he read psychologist John Bowlby's work on the mental health effects of separating children from their mothers – and was inspired to investigate the nature of motherly love among his macaques.

T he position commonly held by psychologists and sociologists is quite clear: The basic motives are, for the most part, the primary drives – particularly hunger, thirst, elimination, pain, and sex – and all other motives, including love or affection, are derived or secondary drives. The mother is associated with the reduction of the primary drives – particularly hunger, thirst, and pain – and through learning, affection or love is derived.

It is entirely reasonable to believe that the

mother through association with food may become a secondary-reinforcing agent, but this is an inadequate mechanism to account for the persistence of the infant-maternal ties . . . Human affection does not extinguish when the mother ceases to have intimate association with the drives in question. Instead, the affectional ties to the mother show a lifelong, unrelenting persistence and, even more surprising, widely expanding generality . . .

The psychoanalysts have concerned themselves with the problem of the nature of the development of love in the neonate and infant, using ill and aging human beings as subjects. They have discovered the overwhelming importance of the breast and related this to the oral erotic tendencies developed at an age preceding their subjects' memories. Their theories range from a belief that the infant has an innate need to achieve and suckle at the breast to beliefs not unlike commonly accepted psychological theories. There are exceptions, as seen in the recent writings of John Bowlby, who attributes importance not only to food and thirst satisfaction, but also to 'primary object-clinging', a need for intimate physical contact, which is initially associated with the mother.

As far as I know, there exists no direct experimental analysis of the relative importance of the stimulus variables determining the affectional or love responses in the neonatal and infant primate.

Unfortunately, the human neonate is a limited experimental subject for such researches because of his inadequate motor capabilities. By the time the human infant's motor responses can be precisely measured, the antecedent determining conditions cannot be defined, having been lost in a jumble and jungle of confounded variables.

Many of these difficulties can be resolved by the use of the neonatal and infant macaque monkey as the subject for the analysis of basic affectional variables. It is possible to make precise measurements in this primate beginning at two to ten days of age, depending upon the maturational status of the individual animal at birth. The macaque infant differs from the human infant in that the monkey is more mature at birth and grows more rapidly; but the basic responses relating to affection, including nursing, contact, clinging, and even visual and auditory exploration, exhibit no fundamental differences in the two species. Even the development of perception, fear, frustration, and learning capability follows very similar sequences in rhesus monkeys and human children.

Three years' experimentation before we started our studies on affection gave us experience with the neonatal monkey. We had separated more than 60 of these animals from their mothers 6 to 12 hours after birth and suckled them on tiny bottles. The infant mortality was only a small fraction of what would have obtained had we let the monkey mothers raise their infants. Our bottle-fed babies were healthier and heavier than monkey-mother-reared infants. We know that we are better monkey mothers than are real monkey mothers thanks to synthetic diets, vitamins, iron extracts, penicillin, chloromycetin, 5% glucose, and constant, tender, loving care.

During the course of these studies we noticed that the laboratory raised babies showed strong attachment to the cloth pads (folded gauze diapers) which were used to cover the hardware-cloth floors of their cages. The infants clung to these pads and engaged in violent temper tantrums when the pads were removed and replaced for sanitary reasons. Such contact-need or responsiveness had been reported previously by Gertrude van Wagenen for the monkey and by Thomas McCulloch and George Haslerud for the chimpanzee and is reminiscent of the devotion often exhibited by human infants to their pillows, blankets, and soft, cuddly stuffed toys. … The baby, human or monkey, if it is to survive, must clutch at more than a straw.

We had also discovered during some allied observational studies that a baby monkey raised on a bare wire-mesh cage floor survives with difficulty, if at all, during the first five days of life. If a wire-mesh cone is introduced, the baby does better; and, if the cone is covered with terry cloth, husky, healthy, happy babies evolve. It takes more than a baby and a box to make a normal monkey. We were impressed by the possibility that, above and beyond the bubbling fountain of breast or bottle, contact comfort might be a very important variable in the development of the infant's affection for the mother.

At this point we decided to study the development of affectional responses of neonatal and infant monkeys to an artificial, inanimate mother, and so we built a surrogate mother which we hoped and believed would be a good surrogate mother. In devising this surrogate mother we were dependent neither upon the capriciousness of evolutionary processes nor upon mutations produced by chance radioactive fallout. Instead, we designed the mother surrogate in terms of modern human engineering principles. We produced a perfectly proportioned, streamlined body stripped of unnecessary bulges and appendices. Redundancy in the surrogate mother's system was avoided by reducing the number of breasts from two to one and placing this unibreast in an upper-thoracic, sagittal position, thus maximizing the natural and known perceptual-motor capabilities of the infant operator. The surrogate was made from a block of wood, covered with sponge rubber, and sheathed in tan cotton terry cloth. A light bulb behind her radiated heat. The result was a mother, soft, warm, and tender, a mother with infinite patience, a mother available twenty-four hours a day, a mother that never scolded her infant and never struck or bit her baby in anger. Furthermore, we designed a mother-machine with maximal maintenance efficiency since failure of any system or function could be resolved by the simple substitution of black boxes and new component parts. It is our opinion that we engineered a very superior monkey mother, although this position is not held universally by the monkey fathers.

Before beginning our initial experiment we also designed and constructed a second mother surrogate, a surrogate in which we deliberately built less than the maximal capability for contact comfort . . . She is made of wire-mesh, a substance entirely adequate to provide postural support and nursing capability, and she is warmed by radiant heat. Her body differs in no essential way from that of the cloth mother surrogate other than in the quality of the contact comfort which she can supply.

In our initial experiment, the dual mother-surrogate condition, a cloth mother and a wire mother were placed in different cubicles attached to the infant's living cage .... For four newborn monkeys the cloth mother lactated and the wire mother did not; and, for the other four, this condition was reversed. In either condition the infant received all its milk through the mother surrogate as soon as it was able to maintain itself in this way, a capability achieved within two or three days except in the case of very immature infants. Supplementary feedings were given until the milk intake from the mother surrogate was adequate. Thus, the experiment was designed as a test of the relative importance of the variables of contact comfort and nursing comfort. During the first 14 days of life the monkey's cage floor was covered with a heating pad wrapped in a folded gauze diaper, and thereafter the cage floor was bare. The infants were always free to leave the heating pad or cage floor to contact either mother, and the time spent on the surrogate mothers was automatically recorded . . . [Our] data make it obvious that contact comfort is a variable of overwhelming importance in the development of affectional response, whereas lactation is a variable of negligible importance. With age and opportunity to learn, subjects with the lactating wire mother showed decreasing responsiveness to her and increasing responsiveness to the nonlactating cloth mother, a finding completely contrary to any interpretation of derived drive in which the mother-form becomes conditioned to hunger-thirst reduction. The persistence of these differential responses throughout 165 consecutive days of testing [was] evident.

One control group of neonatal monkeys was raised on a single wire mother, and a second control group was raised on a single cloth mother. There were no differences between these two groups in amount of milk ingested or in weight gain. The only difference between the two groups lay in the composition of the feces, the softer stools of the wire-mother infants suggesting psychosomatic involvement. The wire mother is biologically adequate but psychologically inept.

We were not surprised to discover that contact comfort was an important basic affectional or love variable, but we did not expect it to overshadow so completely the variable of nursing; indeed, the disparity is so great as to suggest that the primary function of nursing as an affectional variable is that of insuring frequent and intimate body contact of the infant with the mother. Certainly, man cannot live by milk alone. Love is an emotion that does not need to be bottle- or spoon-fed, and we may be sure that there is nothing to be gained by giving lip service to love.

BENJAMIN SPOCK, MD

– *from* Dr Spock Talks with Mothers (1962) –

Before the death of Dr Benjamin Spock (1903–1998), his book *The Common Sense Book of Baby and Child Care* had sold over 50 million copies around the world (in numerous updated editions, of course). Spock opened it with a large dose of reassurance: 'Trust yourself. You know more than you think you do.' He upturned many of the 'scientific' regimes that had dictated feeding times, sleeping times and play times since the 1920s, putting forward the view that raising a child comes somewhat naturally to parents. They just need to show affection.

In *Dr Spock Talks with Mothers*, he answered letters submitted to the monthly magazine *Ladies Home Journal* by mothers seeking counsel on the physical and psychological development of their children. He was fast to note his disdain for the methods under which he was raised – including the idea that cold, fresh air invigorated a child's spirit. He was most animated when describing the mixed messages parents can send unintentionally. Here he pointed out that children learn from what you do, not just from what you say.

'How do I make him mind?' is the most frequent question of some mothers. Actually it's not so much a question, because they don't really expect an answer from the relative or doctor or teacher they are speaking to. It's more a complaint – that the child is unmanageable – and an appeal for agreement and sympathy. Of course we all lose control of our children occasionally, but I want to talk about the few unhappy parents who hardly ever seem to have it, because we can see the issues more clearly in these exaggerated cases.

The answer to such a parent might be another question: 'Do you really mean it, when you ask your child to obey?' The parent would naturally and sincerely say yes, but this would be only partly true. If you or I were watching her during a disciplinary crisis (let's say it's the mother, not because fathers don't have such difficulties but because it's easier to say 'her' for the mother and to pretend that all the bad children are 'he'), we'd probably be able to spot the trouble right away. (If she saw you or me having trouble with our child she'd be able to see how we got off on the wrong foot, too; it's always clearer in the case of somebody else.)

Here are some examples that I've seen first hand:

A doesn't seem to notice when her small child is playing with his milk – comes to only when the whole glass is spilled.

B calls out 'Don't fool with your milk' when she sees the child starting to do just that and then turns away, though there is no evidence that the child has obeyed. She notices again only when the milk goes over.

C gives her boy a slap when she catches him climbing up on the mudguard of the car, but when she sees him doing it again two minutes later she doesn't say or do anything.

D, when her son climbs up on the mudguard again, says – in his hearing – to a friend, 'See, I can't do a thing with him.'

E is heard shouting threats all day long ('I'll put you to bed; I'll call the cops; I'll give you a good hiding'), but as far as the neighbours can see, the threats don't do any good and she never carries out any of them.

F starts to scold her son (for being unpleasant to a neighbour). He turns on her, shouting, 'I don't care, you're nasty.' Surprisingly, she doesn't punish him or seem shocked. She and he keep raising their voices a notch as they holler back and forth until one or the other gets bored and wanders away.

G, leaving her son at kindergarten for the first time, tells the teacher, in front him, 'He's a holy terror.' (The teacher has no trouble with him.)

H's one-year-old wanders innocently into the living room and she says instantly, 'Now don't touch the T.V.' He hadn't thought of it, but now, challenged, he inches towards it while his mother sits still, glaring at him. She turns to a visitor and says, 'See what I mean?'

J, whose father was an alcoholic, asks suspiciously of her sixteen-year-old son, who has been to a party, 'Did you take a drink?' (He didn't.)

The next and last example is a little different, but belongs in our discussion. A first-born baby is brought to K, his mother, for the first time in the hospital, with his thumb in his mouth. She says 'Naughty boy!' – not jokingly but crossly.

Maybe you've become irritated with such a succession of bad examples and think they are too exaggerated, but they're all quite real. They bring out several of the factors that get in the way of good discipline. Parents in situations like these think they are trying to make their children behave, and I am sure that consciously they want them to . . . .

When we are in the right mood and on the right track, we find that we can manage our children without deep thought or great effort. Actually we are using a wide variety of elaborate and delicate methods, but with as little concern as a person who sits down at the piano and plays a piece he learned ten years before. The child does a lot of the work. We know we can depend most of the time on his wanting to please us because he loves us as we love him. As early as one year of age, and most intensively between three and six, he is trying to be grown up like us – in politeness, skilfulness, usefulness. In the school years he strives himself for conformity to the standards set by his friends and the school.

We generally manage our children in their earlier years by example, by positive suggestion, by distraction, by leading by the hand, by appealing to their desire to be grown up, by bodily removal. In the second year, when the child has some sense of what we want and don't want, we all begin gradually to rely more and more on verbal requests and prohibitions. We sense, with whatever leadership qualities we have, that we have to be reasonably consistent (perfection is fortunately not required), feel and speak and act as if we expected to be obeyed, and have at least a touch of friendliness in our tone of voice, such as we'd use in making a request of a friend. The last is the hardest to maintain through a long day. We've carried over enough disapproval from our upbringing so that we easily slip into the tone of irritation, the tone that says 'I don't suppose you'll obey' or 'I've been feeling cross with you and now I'm getting even with you by asking you to do something you don't like (or to stop doing something you enjoy).'

MARVIN J. GERSH, MD

– *from* How to Raise Children at Home in Your Spare Time (1966) –

The paediatrician Dr Marvin Gersh (1922–2005) saw humour in Dr Spock's wild celebrity: if parents were supposed to trust themselves, surely they didn't need to purchase so many tomes telling them how to raise their children? He believed that parents were being made to feel guilty and anxious about how they raised their children when parenthood should instil feelings of fun and joy. His take on baby books included this advice on weaning yourself from them.

After you have had your third or fourth child, you are probably ready to start weaning yourself from baby books. Remember you are not going to succeed right away. It is a good idea to start trying to wean yourself little by little, beginning with your second child. Start with something simple.

Let us say that your baby has spit up a little bit. Naturally you will think back automatically to the section in your baby book on spitting up. You will remember that many babies spit up and that many babies do not, and that some babies spit up once in a while, and some babies spit up every day, and still there are some babies who spit up once in a while for a while and then spit up every day for a while.

You will immediately recognize that your baby is one of the many babies who spit up. It is too soon for you to know whether he is one of the once in a while spitters, or the daily spitters, or the once in a while sometimes daily spitters, or the daily double spitters.

Naturally most spitting up is not serious, but on the other hand, spitting up can be serious if it is not spitting up but it may appear to be spitting up, but actually it may be projectile vomiting, so the section says. Well, if it is projectile vomiting, it may be serious, but since most spitting up is not serious, it probably is not projectile vomiting, but on the other hand, if you are in doubt, you can always call up your pediatrician.

Try to be breezy and cheerful so that the baby does not get the idea that you are upset; after all if you are tense, baby may become tense, and this may cause the baby to spit up. Sometimes spitting up may be emotional, and in some cases it may mean that you are rejecting your baby. Remember we all have unconscious feelings that we do not know about. Sometimes we need the help of a child psychologist, or your local child guidance clinic. Suppose your town does not have a child guidance clinic, and you cannot afford a good child psychologist: try to manage as best you can, and remember a breezy, cheerful and confident attitude is always best. Be firm but try not to be harsh. Remember spitting up is O.K. If it shoots out a foot or two or if spitting up is associated with weight loss, then you should see your doctor. Otherwise, if your baby spits up, just DUCK.

I think you will learn to wean yourself from baby books when you see that sometimes the writer of the book is as scared as you are. His insecurity lies in the fact that he is afraid to reassure you completely lest he lead you to error. You will see in most books on child care that toward the end of each chapter or paragraph on a subject, the author will begin to hedge. He is getting a little insecure too. Consequently, he will almost always add, after reassuring you most of the way, that if there is any doubt you'd best call your doctor. He gets himself off the hook that way, and frankly I think it is unavoidable.

You cannot teach anybody to play golf by the book, much less raise a child by the book. I can see no way out for the parents, other than experience. I have found out that the number of questions asked by parents cuts down progressively as the number of children increases. By the second or third child, you can tell a serious problem from a trivial one. You are consulting your doctor regularly anyway, and things work out quite well. If only we could make our first baby seem like our second.

D. W. WINNICOTT

– *from* The Building Up of Trust (1969) –

British psychoanalyst Donald Woods Winnicott (1896–1971) believed in 'the sound instincts of normal parents' and the ability of parents to create 'stable and healthy families' without special training or counselling. He first described this as the phenomenon of the 'ordinary good mother', in contrast to the idealised 'good mother' prescribed by psychoanalyst Melanie Klein as an antidote to an infant's unconscious anxiety of having bad parents. As he spoke more widely, he put it more plainly: children simply needed 'good enough' parents. And most parents were 'good enough' without much trying.

Winnicott's book *The Child, the Family, and the Outside World* (1964) collected transcripts of a series of talks for mothers and fathers which were broadcast on BBC radio. This piece, which he wrote specifically for parents, was not published until near the end of his career, when he was firmly advocating his 'good enough' approach.

We expect children to have gathered into themselves innumerable samples of good care, and they go forward with a measure of belief, belief in people and in the world, so that it takes quite a big thing to knock them sideways. At the earlier age, however, this belief in things and this trust in people are in process of being built up.

This is the main thing that we notice about the very young, that although they trust us their faith can easily be shattered. For this reason we are especially careful to be reliable in essentials.

It will be understood that we do not do this by deliberate effort or by the study of books or by listening to lectures, but we do it because little children draw the best out of us . . .

Children can understand a great deal so long as a home exists, and the parents are seen together, and if there is warmth even in a cold climate, and food that can be expected and enjoyed, and an absence of the sudden unpredictable noise that hurts physically and cannot be explained away. With physical conditions that can be known and, so to speak, caught hold of, children can stand some strain in the relationship between the parents, since it is, for them, a good thing that at any rate the parents are there, are alive, and have feelings. At the same time it is true that the growth of young children is more easily accomplished if they have parents in an easy relationship the one with the other. Indeed it is the interpersonal world of the parents that is symbolised for the child by the stability of the house and the liveliness of the street . . .

Not Idealism

I must be careful. So easily in describing what very young children need I can seem to be wanting parents to be selfless angels, and expecting the world to be ideal, like a suburban garden in summer with father cutting the grass, and mother preparing the Sunday dinner, and the dog barking at an alien dog over the garden fence. Of children, even babies, it can be said that they do not do well on mechanical perfection. They need human beings around them who both succeed and fail.

I like to use the words 'good enough'. Good enough parents can be used by babies and young children, and good enough means you and me. In order to be consistent, and so to be predictable for our children, we must be *ourselves*. If we are ourselves our children can get to know us. Certainly if we are acting a part we shall be found out when we get caught without our make-up . . .

What to Know

What is it, then, that parents can usefully know? I would suggest that there are two main things to know, one of which has to do with the process of growth, which belongs to the child, and the other has to do with the environmental provisions, which is very much your responsibility.

The process of growth

Once it has been pointed out to you it is surely quite obvious that your baby has a tendency to live and breathe and to eat and drink, and to grow. You will be wise if you assume these matters to be true from the very beginning.

It helps a lot to know that you do not have to make your baby into a child, to make your child grow, to make your growing child good or clean, to make your good child generous, to make your generous child clever at choosing the right presents for the right people.

If you stand back and watch you soon see the developmental process at work, and you get a sense of relief. You have started up something that has its own built-in dynamo. You will be looking for the brakes.

Every comment I make must be modified by the other observation, which is that no two children are alike, so that you may find yourself bothered by one child's lifelessness and by another child's dynamism. But the main principle holds in all cases, that it is the child's own developmental processes that make the changes you are looking for.

So the first useful principle has to do with the innate tendencies that belong to each young child.

The environment

The second useful principle has to do with your special place as the environment and as the provider of environment. No-one has to prove to you that a baby needs gentle handling and warmth after being born. You know it to be true. If someone doubts this it is for him or her to prove that what you know is wrong.

After all, you have been a baby yourself, and you have memories to guide you, apart from all you may have learned when watching and participating in the care of babies.

The environment you provide is primarily yourself, your person, your nature, your distinguishing features that help you know you are yourself. This includes of course all that you collect around yourself, your aroma, the atmosphere that goes with you, and it includes the man who will turn out to be the baby's father, and it may include other children if you have them, as well as grandparents and aunts and uncles. In other words, I am doing no more than describe the family as the baby gradually discovers it, including the features of the home that make your home not quite like any other home . . .

Your child playing under the table stands up and the table hits his head. He rushes to you and prepares for a good cry. You make appropriate noises and put your hand where the head got hurt, and perhaps you mend it with a kiss. After a few minutes all is well, and play under the table is resumed. What would have been the gain if you had been able to write a thesis on various aspects of this event?

1. This is the way children learn while they are play-ing. They must look before they leap . . .
2. The table did not really hit the child's head, but at that age the first assumption will be of that kind, and one child is more likely than another to cling on to the 'persecution' theory of trauma; this has to do with a difficulty in accepting the fact of one's own aggression, and perhaps with rage that became lost because of its painfulness as an expe-rience for a baby or small child who is not yet sure of keeping integrated when powerful emotion is roused . . .
3. Would this be a good moment for giving a lec-ture: 'You see, if you move about like that without thinking you will hurt yourself, and one day . . .'

No, I think it is better when the whole matter is sealed off with a healing kiss, simply because you know what you would be feeling like if you were that little child who has been hit on the head by a nasty hard vindictive table . . .

The environmental provision

For babies and young children the environmental provision either gives a chance for the internal process of growth to take place or else it presents this very thing.

The key word could be 'predictability'. Parents, and especially the mother at the start, are taking a lot of trouble to shield the child from that which is unpredictable.

It will be seen that at a quick or slow pace this or that child is becoming able to put two and two together and to defeat unpredictability. There is an amazing variation here, according to the small child's capacity to defeat unpredictability. But there remains the need for mother. An aeroplane flies low overhead. This can be hurtful even to an adult. No explanation is valuable for the child. What is valuable is that you hold the child close to yourself, and the child uses the fact that you are not scared beyond recovery, and is soon off and away, playing again. Had you not been there the child could have been hurt beyond repair.

This is a crude example, but I am showing that by this way of looking at child care, stress can be described in terms of failure of environmental provision, just where reliability is needed.

It is the same thing when a mother must leave a little child in a hospital for a few days, as has been emphasized by [John] Bowlby, and also by James and Joyce Robertson in their poignant film *A Two-Year-Old Goes to Hospital.* By this age the child has really come to know the mother as a person, and it is herself that he must have, not just her care and protection. Stress at this age comes from the fact that the mother is absent over a period of time that is longer than that over which the child can keep alive the mental image of the mother, or can feel her live presence in the imaginative world of dream and play . . .

It is always the same: there was good enough environmental provision in terms of predictability, according to the child's ability to predict, and then there was an unreliability that automatically broke up the continuity of the child's developmental process. After this the child has a gap in the line between now and the roots of the past. There has to be a new start. Too many of these new starts result in a failure in the child of the feeling *I am, this is me, I exist, it is I who love and hate, it is me that people see and that I see in mother's face when she comes, or in the mirror . . .*

This brings me to the last point, which is that even this matter of environmental provision, reliability, adaptation to infant needs, does not need to be learnt. There is something about having a baby (even preparing for adopting a baby) that alters the parents.

TONI MORRISON

– *from* A World of Ideas (1989) –

Toni Morrison (1931–2019) was awarded the Nobel Prize in Literature in 1993. Her 1987 novel, *Beloved*, was based on a newspaper story she read about Margaret Garner, a woman who had escaped slavery in the South in 1856 and made a home in Ohio. When Garner realised that US marshals had tracked her down and intended to arrest her and her children and return them to slavery, she was compelled to try to save her children from this unspeakable cruelty by killing them. Garner succeeded in killing her youngest, who was just two years old. Morrison imagined that one of the cruelties that Garner thought was too much to bear was the separation of enslaved mothers from their children.

In an interview two years after the novel's publication, Morrison ruminated on motherhood.

With *Beloved*, I began to think about, really, *motherhood*. It's not the all-encompassing role for women now; it can be a secondary role, or you don't have to choose it. But on the other hand, there was something so valuable about what happens when one becomes a mother.

For me, it was the most liberating thing that ever happened to me, having children . . . Because of – the demands the children make are not the demands of a normal 'other'. The children's demands on me were things that nobody else ever asked me to do.

Be a good manager; have a sense of humour; deliver something that somebody can use. And they were not interested in all the things that other people were interested in, like what I was wearing, or, you know, if I was sensual, or if I was – you know, all of that went by . . . They don't want to hear it. They want to know, What are you going to do *now*, *today*? And somehow, all of the baggage that I had accumulated as a person about what was valuable, so much of that just fell away. And I could not only be me, whatever that was; somebody actually needed me to be that. It's different from being a daughter. ...

If you listen to them, somehow you are able to free yourself from baggage and vanity and all sorts of things and deliver a better self, one that you like. The person that was in me, that I liked best, was the one my children seemed to want.

NAOMI STADLEN

– *from* What Mothers Do (2004) –

After her three children were at school, Naomi Stadlen (b. 1942) trained to be a breastfeeding counsellor, working for the National Childbirth Trust, the Active Birth Centre and La Leche League GB. In 1990 she started to host a weekly discussion group for mothers which evolved into Mothers Talking, a place where mothers may speak openly and safely about the multitude of choices they make when raising their children. Her book *What Mothers Do* grew out of her observations that all mothers share one thing – love for their children. This gift of love invests their feelings of responsibility and uncertainty, their constant state of vigilance and, often, their irritability. It's also seen in their power to comfort.

A whole genre of books has developed that pressure mothers to follow the authors' personal rules or guidelines, because these are supposed to make motherhood easier. But how useful is a programme of rules? Mothers who try to follow such rules often react by complaining that looking after a baby is dreadfully boring. This is understandable. If one is following a set of rules, looking after a baby definitely gets boring. Each individual baby is sure to seem abnormal. He is unlikely to fit any particular set of rules – which were presumably based on the needs of a completely different baby. One can easily lose the joy of getting to know someone wholly unique.

After the birth of my daughter, I looked around to find other mothers who had made the same choices that I had. But of course no one else had. Instead, we had each made some important post-natal decisions. We had chosen whether to breastfeed or to use formula feeds; which nappies to use; whether to use a cot or to sleep with the baby; carry the baby in a sling or wheel him in a pushchair; sleep-train or not; cuddle a crying baby or leave him to cry; vaccinate the baby and, if so, which vaccines to use, in which combinations and when; use conventional or 'alternative' medicine; employ professional childcare and, if so, which kind . . . and more. It still alarms me to think about this list. Every choice opens up into many smaller choices. We live in a tolerant society, and choice is a valuable consequence of this. However, mothers often feel categorised by their choices, and cut off from other mothers who have chosen differently.

Understandably, mothers can then become defensive. I found that conversations with other mothers would often turn into competitions. One mother might say: 'My baby eats more solids/sleeps longer/is more active than other babies of his age.' 'Top that!' is the silent challenge to other mothers. In a different kind of competition, mothers vie with each other about who is the 'expert'. 'I'll tell you what *I* used for colic,' one mother tells another. There is a note of authoritative command in her voice. A third sort of conversation might sound more relaxed because it includes story-telling and laughter. But the tension runs just below the surface. The bottom line is 'I'm having a much more horrible time as a mother than you are.' This sort of competition is for the jackpot of maximum sympathy from all the listening mothers.

Yet it doesn't have to be like this. Motherhood is not a competition. There's room for every one of us. Motherhood is huge. No one could ever fulfil all its possibilities. No one could ever make entirely good choices. All of us have times of failure. Surely no mother could ever be a total failure either. There is scope for every mother to be good at something. She can then respect other mothers, and feel she belongs *with* them, rather than feel in competition *against* them. Overall, being a mother is a humbling experience. There is always more to learn. Just when her child passes a particular stage, a mother is sure to hear about something much better and simpler that she could have done.

I didn't realise how competitive my conversations with other mothers were. I used to come away feeling bruised, without understanding why. Slowly, I learned that each of us was unique. It was pointless to try to find another me. Instead, I began to listen to all the mothers I met in a more open-minded way.

It was fascinating to see how we all differed. Most mothers had precise reasons for their choices. Their situations were unique. Paradoxically, it was when I listened to the details of mothers' individual situations that I was able to see how much we all shared.

The Power of Comfort

Human comfort is one of the finest strengths that we offer each other. It can be casually given, by a touch, a smile, a few words or even by silence. Yet it's very effective. It doesn't usually alter the source of our troubles, but it strengthens us so we feel better able to confront them.

Many mothers comfort their babies when they cry. This often goes unnoticed. The mother of a baby who cries a lot usually receives pity for being disturbed. She will be perceived as 'unlucky' because her baby needs her so much. Her new ability to comfort is frequently overlooked. This . . . is not meant to pressure anyone into comforting, but to increase our sensitivity to those who do.

Comfort seems to work cumulatively, which means that it is hardest to give at the beginning. Newborns, especially, seem to live mostly in the present moment. When they cry it sounds intensely in the present, and that makes it hard to deal with. Any of us can cry 'like a baby', but however hard we cry we can eventually get back our adult perspective, and it calms us. A newborn, on the other hand, hasn't discovered this yet.

The immediacy of a baby's cry is powerful. This has a practical advantage. A baby needs to be able to alert his mother, since his daily – and nightly – survival depends on her. Which one of us would waken from the depths of sleep, night after night, if our babies didn't insist on it? So we rouse ourselves, remember that we are mothers and become alert. The crying demands that we do something about it.

The literature on crying babies tends to focus on technique. However, responding to a crying baby involves more than technique. Underlying what a mother does is her philosophy of human nature. She may hardly be aware of it, but it affects the many quick decisions she has to make. Her basic choice is either to see her baby as good, in which case she trusts him, or alternatively to see him as the product of evil human nature, or of original sin, which requires her to train him. This makes a great difference.

The mother who trusts her baby will pick him up and hold him close. The mother who sees her baby's crying as cue for training will keep a distance. It can help if a mother who responds one way can appreciate that a mother doing the opposite is not ignorant or short-sighted. It's simply that the two mothers do not share the same basic philosophy. Once they recognise this, mothers can still reach out to each other in understanding. Not all mothers have a clear-cut philosophy. Some aren't sure what they believe. They try first one way and then the other . . .

The mother who is training her baby usually gets much quicker results than the one who trusts hers. The trained baby will soon learn the consistent rules that this mother has laid down. This means that his mother's life will be more predictable and ordered . . . By contrast, the mother who trusts her baby can feel thrown into chaos. Days and nights have lost their shape. Nothing seems predictable . . .

Mothers are quick to discover that babies respond to particular comforting actions. 'Already by the second week,' observed Judy Dunn in her unique book *Distress and Comfort*, 'we find that the human voice is more effective at calming a crying baby than a rattle or a ball.' A mother's ability to provide comfort has been recorded since ancient times. 'As a mother comforts her child,' wrote the biblical prophet Isaiah, who lived in the eighth century BC. For centuries, people have noted how adults in extremes of pain or under torture would cry out for the comfort of their mothers. Even recent social research demonstrates that people feel calmed by a woman's smile and nod, whereas a man behaving in the same way arouses anxiety.

How strange, then, that so *little* has been written about learning to comfort. No one supports the mother while she is learning how to comfort, or celebrates her when she is able to give it. People ask mothers: 'Is he sleeping through the night yet?' 'Have you started him on solids yet?' 'Has he got any teeth?' No one seems to ask: 'Have you discovered what comforts him?' Yet the ability to sleep through the night, or to digest solid food or to grow teeth, has little to do with mothering. Babies reach these milestones when they are mature enough, whereas being able to comfort depends on a mother's ability.

Invariably, a mother starts from the uncertainty of *not* knowing how to comfort. Each new child is an unknown person. If she has several children, she discovers that she has to adapt to each child. The mother of twin girls remembered that she couldn't hold them both in the same way. 'Rachel liked to bounce and Grace liked to sway,' she observed. A mother of twin boys commented that one was comforted by being swaddled, while the other liked to move freely. It takes time to work all this out.

Imagine a toddler falling down in a playground and starting to cry. 'He needs his mum,' everyone agrees, and they lift him, sobbing, into his mother's arms. He is wailing. Huge hot tears roll down his flushed cheeks. His mother rocks him for a moment and strokes his back, and the child starts to relax and calm down. 'Better now?' asks his mother, simultaneously checking him for injury. He gives a wavering smile, then a steadier one, and nods his head.

Off he goes to continue playing. This wonderful transformation took only a few minutes. Whatever did this mother do?

It is clearly not the first time she has comforted him. The whole process depends on both mother and child recalling earlier times. Yet, if you could rewind an imaginary video right back to the start, when the toddler was just newborn, and if you studied the images closely, you would be unlikely to see the mother comforting the child so efficiently. She would probably be in that difficult but important state of motherly uncertainty. Her baby is crying and distressed – and she simply does not know what to do . . .

I have searched the literature for accounts of comforting, but there is extraordinarily little available. Several studies have been written on 'soothing'. But this seems to mean helping the baby to stop crying. Comforting goes further. The mother is not just trying to change her baby's behaviour. She feels compassionate towards his distress, and she wishes she could help. The word *comfort* derives from the Latin word *fortitude*, which means 'strength'. Mothers use their compassion to find ways of helping to restore their babies to a sense of strength.

LYDIA DAVIS

– *from* What You Learn About the Baby (2007) –

Lydia Davis (b. 1947) is widely considered the master of the short story. More so, she has developed 'a literary form largely of her own invention' which straddles prose and poetry, with some of her stories fully told in a single sentence. Several of her meditations on raising an infant fall into this category. Of this piece, the *New York Times* reviewer said: 'Davis's incantatory sentences seem to show a being who has transcended limits in his very awareness of limits, which leads us to think that growing up is largely a measure of how far we stray from that first, initial perfection.'

You Will Not Know What Is Wrong

The baby is on his back in his cradle crying. His legs are slightly lifted from the surface of his mattress in the effort of his crying. His head is so heavy and his legs so light and his muscles so hard that his legs fly up easily from the mattress when he tenses, as now.

Often, you will wonder what is wrong, why he is crying, and it would help, it would save you much disturbance, to know what is wrong, whether he is hungry, or tired, or bored, or cold, or hot, or uncom-

131

fortable in his clothes, or in pain in his stomach or bowels. But you will not know, or not when it would help to know, at the time, but only later, when you have guessed correctly or many times incorrectly. And it will not help to know afterwards, or it will not help unless you have learned from the experience to identify a particular cry that means hunger, or pain, etc. But the memory of a cry is a difficult one to fix in your mind.

What Exhausts You

You must think and feel for him as well as for yourself – that he is tired, or bored, or uncomfortable.

Sitting Still

You learn to sit still. You learn to stare as he stares, to stare up at the rafters as long as he stares up at the rafters, sitting still in a large space.

Entertainment

For him, though not usually for you, merely to look at a thing is an entertainment.

Then, there are some things that not just you, and not just he, but both of you like to do, such as lie in the hammock, or take a walk, or take a bath.

THE ONION

– Study Finds Every Style of Parenting Produces Disturbed Adults (2011) –

When the historian Julia Wrigley surveyed a large corpus of parenting articles in magazines dating from 1900 to 1990, she observed a marked shift from medical advice – more than 60% in 1901 to 1910 – to advice about intellectual development – about 45% from 1961 to 1980. She summarised the evolution: 'The baby of the early decades of the 1900s, presented as a passive, inert being, sleeping most of the day, was gone; in its place was a baby who learned from every touch, every word, every sound, and every smell.'

So it's not surprising that the editors of the online satirical magazine *The Onion* took aim at parenting advice, which had grown into an industry – with parents increasingly told they need to take deep and personal responsibility for their child's cognitive development as well as their physical and emotional health.

A study released by the California Parenting Institute Tuesday shows that every style of parenting inevitably causes children to grow into profoundly unhappy adults. 'Our research suggests that while overprotective parenting ultimately produces adults unprepared to contend with life's difficulties, highly permissive parenting leads to feelings of bitterness and isolation throughout adulthood,' lead researcher Daniel Porter said. 'And, interestingly, we found that anything between those two extremes is equally damaging, always resulting in an adult who suffers from some debilitating combination of unpreparedness and isolation. Despite great variance in parenting styles across populations, the end product is always the same: a profoundly flawed and joyless human being.' The study did find, however, that adults often achieve temporary happiness when they have children of their own to perpetuate the cycle of human misery.

ALISON GOPNIK

– *from* The Gardener and the Carpenter (2016) –

The psychologist and philosopher Alison Gopnik (b. 1955) studies how people learn, particularly during the early years of life. She likens the infant's mind to the scientist's: babies experiment with things around them to build up a mental model of how the world works. That includes dropping peas from their bowl to the ground, over and over, to understand and test the natural law of gravity.

Gopnik argues that creating spaces where children can explore is the parent's most important job in ensuring their child's development. In *The Gardener and the Carpenter*, she explains this change in perspective from the success-oriented model of much modern parenting.

Why be a parent? Taking care of children is demanding and exhausting, and yet for most of us it is also profoundly satisfying. Why? What makes it all worthwhile?

A common answer, especially for middle-class fathers and mothers today, is that you are a parent so that you can do something called 'parenting'. 'To parent' is a goal-directed verb; it describes a job, a kind of work. The goal is to somehow turn your child into a better or happier or more successful adult – better than they would be otherwise, or (though we whisper this) better than the other children next door. The right kind of parenting will produce the right kind of child, who in turn will become the right kind of adult . . .

Working to achieve a particular outcome *is* a good model for many crucial human enterprises. It's the right model for carpenters or writers or businessmen. You can judge whether you are a good carpenter or writer or CEO by the quality of your chairs, your books, or your bottom line. In the parenting picture, parenting follows the same model. A parent is a kind of carpenter; however, the goal is not to produce a particular kind of product, like a chair, but a particular kind of person.

In work, expertise leads to success. The promise of parenting is that there is some set of techniques, some particular expertise, that parents could acquire that would help them accomplish the goal of shaping their children's lives. And a sizable industry has emerged that promises to provide exactly that expertise. Some sixty thousand books are in the parenting section on Amazon, and most of them have 'How to' somewhere in the title.

Many of the parenting how-to books, of course, simply give practical advice about being a parent. But many more promise that if parents just practice the right techniques, they can make a substantial difference in the way their child turns out . . .

From Parenting to Being a Parent

If parenting is the wrong model, what's the right one? 'Parent' is not actually a verb, not a form of work, and it isn't and shouldn't be directed toward the goal of sculpting a child into a particular kind of adult. Instead, to be a parent – to care for a child – is to be part of a profound and unique human relationship, to engage in a particular kind of love. Work is central to human life; we couldn't do without it. But as Freud and Elvis both remarked, apocryphally at least, work *and* love are the two things that make life worthwhile.

The particular love that goes with caring for children is not just restricted to biological mothers and fathers, but includes all the people whom academics call caregivers and the British, more elegantly, just refer to as 'carers'. It's a form of love that is not limited to biological parents, but is at least potentially part of the lives of us all.

We recognize the difference between work and other relationships, other kinds of love. To be a wife is not to engage in 'wifing', to be a friend is not to 'friend', even on Facebook, and we don't 'child' our mothers and fathers. Yet these relationships are central to who we are. Any human being living a fully satisfied life is immersed in such social connections. And this is not only a philosophical truth about human beings, but one that is deeply rooted in our very biology.

Talking about love, especially the love of parents for children, may sound sentimental and mushy, and also simple and obvious. But like all human relationships, the love of children is at once a part of the everyday texture of our lives – ubiquitous, inescapable, and in the background of everything we do – and enormously complicated, variable, and even paradoxical.

We can aspire to love better without thinking of love as a kind of work. We might say that we try hard to be a good wife or husband, or that it's important to us to be a good friend or a better child. But I would not evaluate the success of my marriage by measuring whether my husband's character had improved in the years since we wed. I would not evaluate the quality of an old friendship by whether my friend was happier or more successful than when we first met – indeed, we all know that friendships show their quality most in the darkest days. Nevertheless, this is the implicit picture of parenting – that your qualities as a parent can be, and even should be, judged by the child you create . . .

Love doesn't have goals or benchmarks or blueprints, but it does have a purpose. The purpose is not to change the people we love, but to give them what they need to thrive. Love's purpose is not to shape our beloved's destiny, but to help them to shape their own. It isn't to show them the way, but to help them find a path for themselves, even if the path they take isn't one we would choose ourselves, or even one we would choose for them.

The purpose of loving children, in particular, is to give those helpless young human beings a rich, stable, safe environment – an environment in which variation, innovation, and novelty can blossom . . .

The Child Garden

Perhaps the best metaphor of all for understanding our distinctive relationship to children is an old one. Caring for children is like tending a garden, and being a parent is like being a gardener.

In the parenting model, being a parent is like being a carpenter. You should pay some attention to the kind of material you are working with, and it may have some influence on what you try to do. But essentially your job is to shape that material into a final product that will fit the scheme you had in mind to begin with. And you can assess how good a job you've done by looking at the finished product. Are the doors true? Are the chairs steady? Messiness and variability are a carpenter's enemies; precision and control are her allies. Measure twice, cut once.

When we garden, on the other hand, we create a protected and nurturing space for plants to flourish. It takes hard labor and the sweat of our brows, with a lot of exhausted digging and wallowing in manure. And as any gardener knows, our specific plans are always thwarted. The poppy comes up neon orange instead of pale pink, the rose that was supposed to climb the fence stubbornly remains a foot from the ground, black spot and rust and aphids can never be defeated.

And yet the compensation is that our greatest horticultural triumphs and joys also come when the garden escapes our control, when the weedy white Queen Anne's lace unexpectedly shows up in just the right place in front of the dark yew tree, when the forgotten daffodil travels to the other side of the garden and busts out among the blue forget-me-nots, when the grapevine that was supposed to stay demurely hitched to the arbor runs scarlet riot through the trees.

In fact, there is a deeper sense in which such accidents are a hallmark of good gardening. There are admittedly some kinds of gardening where the aim is a particular outcome, like growing hothouse orchids or training bonsai trees. Those kinds of gardening demand the same sort of admirable expertise and skill as fine carpentry. In England, that land of gardeners, they use the term 'hothousing' to refer to the kind of anxious middle-class parenting that Americans call 'helicoptering'.

But consider creating a meadow or a hedgerow or a cottage garden. The glory of a meadow is its messiness – the different grasses and flowers may flourish or perish as circumstances alter, and there is no guarantee that any individual plant will become the tallest, or fairest, or most long-blooming. The good gardener works to create fertile soil that can sustain a whole ecosystem of different plants with different strengths and beauties – and with different weaknesses and difficulties, too. Unlike a good chair, a good garden is constantly changing, as it adapts to the changing circumstances of the weather and the seasons. And in the long run, that kind of varied, flexible, complex, dynamic system will be more robust and adaptable than the most carefully tended hothouse bloom.

Being a good parent won't transform children into smart or happy or successful adults. But it can help create a new generation that is more robust and adaptable and resilient, better able to deal with the inevitable, unpredictable changes that face them in the future.

Gardening is risky and often heartbreaking. Every gardener knows the pain of watching that most promising of sprouts wither unexpectedly. But the only garden that didn't have those risks, that wasn't attended with that pain, would be one made of Astroturf studded with plastic daisies. ...

So our job as parents is not to make a particular kind of child. Instead, our job is to provide a protected space of love, safety, and stability in which children of many unpredictable kinds can flourish.

Our job is not to shape our children's minds; it's to let those minds explore all the possibilities that the world allows. Our job is not to tell children how to play; it's to give them the toys and pick the toys up again after the kids are done. We can't make children learn, but we can let them learn.

GIUSEPPINA PERSICO *et al.*

– *from* Maternal Singing of Lullabies (2017) –

Like fairy tales, lullabies are found around the world and across the ages. The oldest lullaby discovered thus far – 'Little Baby in the Dark House', as translated from the original Babylonian cuneiform – is four thousand years old.

When the Spanish poet Frederico García Lorca studied lullabies in the 1920s, he noticed that many were filled with stories of sadness. He hypothesised that a mother could express fears and anxiety for her child through a lullaby while simultaneously soothing her infant. The sounds were comforting, the words not yet intelligible. The findings in 'Maternal Singing of Lullabies' appear to support Lorca's hypothesis.

From conception to birth, all human beings establish a relationship with their mother that allows them to interact with her. The mother-infant relationship starts during pregnancy when the mother perceives foetal movements, and from then on a special dialogue develops between mother and baby. This bonding is further strengthened at the moment of childbirth. After pregnancy, the relationship between mother and baby has a special channel of communication: the maternal voice.

The auditory foetal system already reaches full maturity between the 24th and 28th weeks' gestation. From this moment the foetus is able to react to auditory stimuli. Kisilevsky et al. investigated foetal responses to music played with a headset placed on the maternal abdomen and found an increase in foetal motor activity and in foetal heart rate in the foetus from 28 weeks. Among all the acoustic signals perceived during pregnancy, the maternal voice is the predominant one and the main source of sensory stimulation.

From the 28th to the 36th week, the phenomenon of 'habituation' occurs: the foetus is able to preserve the sound memory of the vibro-acoustic stimuli to which it is repeatedly exposed. This is one of the most important higher brain functions involving learning and ability to retrieve information. Some authors have suggested that the newborn recognises and responds positively to the maternal voice as a result of prenatal exposure, and is soothed when exposed to the same stimulus in the early postnatal period. The sound experience during the prenatal period is so incisive that after birth a newborn is able to discriminate between maternal and other female voices and demonstrates a clear preference for the former . . .

An interesting form of acoustic communication between the mother and child is represented by maternal singing in pregnancy which is an important precursor for the relationship. Even after birth, maternal singing to the infant is an expression of maternal love and is generally recognised as being beneficial for both mother and newborn. Lullabies are differentiated from other types of songs due to their repetitiveness, soothing quality, softness, simplicity and slow tempo . . .

This study aims to explore the potential of maternal singing of lullabies . . . The choice of lullabies, as opposed to other kinds of music, is a result of their communicative value and their importance as one of the symbols of mother-infant relationships in all cultures around the world . . .

A remarkable percentage of women (90.6%) reported positive emotions after singing, such as: serenity, relaxation or a feeling of being on the same wavelength as their baby. At one month after birth, mothers continued singing lullabies, especially when the baby was fidgety (42%), cried (3.7%), went to sleep (32%) or during play time and cuddling (15%) . . . Perceived maternal stress at one month was reduced in the singing cohort in terms of ease of going back to sleep after an awakening (29.6% for the singing cohort vs 36.5% for the concurrent cohort).

Mothers in the singing group unanimously emphasised the strong emotions and feelings they experienced while singing, both in pregnancy and after birth [and] maternal singing of lullabies can improve mother-infant bonding.

BERNADINE EVARISTO

– *from* Girl, Woman, Other (2019) –

When Bernardine Evaristo (b. 1959) won the Booker Prize for *Girl, Woman, Other*, she was the first Black woman to win it. The freedom with which the character of Amma raises her daughter, Yazz, stands in stark contrast to Evaristo's memories of her own childhood: 'I grew up with a father who was quite patriarchal in the way he raised his children. He was a very strict disciplinarian,' she said. 'I'm not being critical of him because I understand fully . . . But it felt quite oppressive.'

In 2022, Evaristo was appointed president of the Royal Society of Literature.

Yazz

was born nineteen years ago in a birthing pool in Amma's candelit living room

surrounded by incense, the music of lapping waves, a doula *and* a midwife, Shirley and Roland – her great friend, who'd agreed to father her child when the death of her parents triggered an unprecedented and all-consuming broodiness

luckily for her, Roland, five years into his partnership with Kenny, had also been thinking about fatherhood

he took Yazz every other weekend, as agreed, which Amma regretted when she found herself missing her newborn instead of feeling deliriously free from Friday afternoons to Sunday evenings
Yazz was the miracle she never thought she wanted, and having a child really did complete her, something she rarely confided because it somehow seemed anti-feminist
Yazz was going to be her countercultural experiment

she breastfed her wherever she happened to be, and didn't care who was offended at a mother's need to feed her child
she took her everywhere, strapped to her back or across her front in a sling, deposited her in the corner of rehearsal rooms, or on the table at meetings
she took her on tour on trains and planes in a travel cot that looked more like a carry-all, once almost sending her through the airport scanner, begging them not to arrest her over it
she created the position of seven godmothers and two godfathers
to ensure there'd be a supply of babysitters for when her child was no longer quite so compliant and portable

Yazz was allowed to wear exactly what she liked so long as she wasn't endangering herself or her health she wanted her to be self-expressed before they tried to crush her child's free spirit through the oppressive regimentation of the education system

she has a photo of her daughter walking down the street wearing a plastic Roman army breastplate over an orange tutu, white fairy wings, a pair of yellow shorts over red and white stripy leggings, a different shoe on each foot (a sandal and a welly), lipstick smudged on her lips, cheeks and forehead (a phase), and her hair tied into an assortment of bunches with miniature dolls hanging off the ends

Amma ignored the pitying or judgemental looks from passers-by and small-minded mothers at the playground or nursery

Yazz was never told off for speaking her mind, although she was told off for swearing because she needed to develop her vocabulary

(Yazz, say you find Marissa unpleasant or unlikeable rather than describing her as a shit-faced smelly bottom)

PERMISSIONS